The Workbook on

Keeping Company

with the

Saints

Maxie Dunnam

UPPER ROOM BOOKS®
NASHVILLE

The Upper Room® Web site: http://www.upperroom.org

UPPER ROOM®, UPPER ROOM BOOKS® and design logos are trademarks owned by the Upper Room®, Nashville, Tennessee. All rights reserved.

Scripture quotations not otherwise identified are from the New Revised Standard Version of the Bible, copyright © 1989 by the Division of Christian Education of the National Council of the Churches of Christ in the USA and are used by permission.

Scripture quotations designated KJV are from the King James Version.

Scripture quotations noted NKJV are from the New King James Version. Copyright © 1979, 1980, 1982 Thomas Nelson, Inc., Publishers.

Scripture quotations designated JBPHILLIPS are from *The New Testament in Modern English*, © J. B. Phillips 1958. Used by permission of the Macmillan Company.

Scripture quotations designated NEB are from the New English Bible. © The delegates of the Oxford University Press and the Syndics of the Cambridge University Press 1961, 1970. Reprinted by permission.

Scripture quotations designated NIV are from the Holy Bible, New International Version. Copyright © 1973, 1978, 1984 International Bible Society. Used by permission of Zondervan Bible Publishers.

Scripture quotations designated RSV are from the Revised Standard Version of the Bible, copyrighted 1946, 1952, and ©1971 by the Division of Christian Education, National Council of Churches of Christ in USA. Used by permission.

Scripture quotation from *The Living Bible* (Wheaton, Illinois: Tyndale House Publishers, 1971) is used by permission.

Scripture quotations designated THE MESSAGE are from The Message: New Testament with Psalms and Proverbs by Eugene H. Peterson, Copyright © 1993, 1994, 1995 NavPress Publishing Group. All rights reserved.

Scripture quotation designated WEYMOUTH is from *The New Testament in Modern Speech* by Richard Francis Weymouth. New York: Harper & Brothers/London: James Clarke & Company.

Scripture noted NASB is from the New American Standard Bible, © The Lockman Foundation 1960, 1962, 1968, 1971, 1973, 1975, 1977.

Please see page 205 for additional acknowledgments.

Cover design: John Robinson
Cover photograph: © William A. Bake/CORBIS
Interior design: Nancy J. Cole
First printing: 2001

Library of Congress Cataloging-in-Publication Data

Dunnam, Maxie D.
    The workbook on keeping company with the saints / by Maxie D. Dunnam
        p. cm.
    ISBN 0-8358-0925-0
        1. Spiritual life—Christianity. 2. Christian saints—Biography. 3. Spiritual life—Methodist Church. I. Title.

BV4501.2.D775 2001
248.4‑ ‑dc21   2001017871

Printed in the United States of America.

To our grandchildren,
Nathan, Maggie, Hannah and Jacob,
Gifts from God—full of Life
I pray you will begin early and always to keep company with the saints.

Contents

Introduction

I have been on my Christian journey in an intentional way since my conversion and public profession of faith at age thirteen. That journey took on deeper dimensions when I answered the call to preach at age seventeen. I was actually appointed as pastor of three congregations on what we Methodists call a "circuit" when I was nineteen. Bless the people in those three congregations! They were obviously patient and long-suffering, and they provided caring support for a fledgling preacher of the gospel. I served those three churches during my last two years of college before going to Candler School of Theology, Emory University, for graduate study and specific preparation for ministry.

A number of events and crucial time frames in my ministry were watershed occasions, transition times, marking a dramatic redirection or paradigm shift in my understanding of vocation, church, Christian life, and spirituality. One of these came when I was four years out of seminary. I had been the founding pastor of a new congregation in Gulfport, Mississippi. It was a marvelous opportunity for church growth and ministry. The congregation grew rapidly; it became a kind of "Cinderella congregation." We built new buildings, took in many members, and had an active suburban church life.

On the surface, the situation could not have been better. But behind the scenes turbulent events were affecting us all. The civil rights movement was in full swing, and every Christian congregation, especially in the South, was caught in the tension such issues inevitably bring.

In the midst of that ministry, it became apparent that something was missing from my life, and certainly something was missing from the life of the congregation. There was little difference, if any, between the attitudes of people within and those outside the church. The pressure on me as the minister and the resulting internal turmoil and tension was, to say the least, totally energy-draining. The truth of the matter is, I did not have the spiritual resources to cope.

I had begun to bring people together in small prayer-and-study groups, believing that only through an intentional, spiritually disciplined life could we make the kinds of decisions we needed to make, relating to one another within and outside the congregation in a Christlike fashion. One of the books we used for our reflection and growth was E. Stanley Jones's *In Christ*. This book became a monumental help for me, and though I was not aware of it then, it became one of the most important resources in my spiritual journey.

At a time when the temptation to "throw in the towel" was exceedingly great, I providentially responded to an invitation to attend an E. Stanley Jones Christian ashram. Stanley Jones had adapted the ashram from the Hindu culture as a model for a spiritual growth movement that spread around the world. Spending a week of study, prayer, physical work, and reflection under the direction of Brother Stanley was one of those significant shaping times of my life. I rededicated my life to Christ, recommitted myself to ministry, and I realized that my personal Christian life and ministry were dependent upon an intentional, disciplined life of spiritual growth, seeking to be yielded completely to the indwelling Christ.

My life and ministry took a marked turn. Prayer and scripture study became more the center of my life than ever before. I began to structure the congregation around study, prayer, and sharing groups where people became accountable to one another for spiritual growth.

The civil rights movement and the turmoil and tension within the church swirling around its issues took their toll on a number of young Methodist ministers. As a result of that strain and our feeling that we were receiving absolutely no support from church leadership, a number of us left Mississippi. I went to California and continued my ministry there—still believing that individuals and congregations were to be shaped by deliberate, intentional, spiritual discipline. Out of that ongoing commitment came another specific reshaping, redirecting occasion in my life. I was invited to join the staff of The Upper Room to direct a ministry, primarily calling people to a life of prayer, providing direction and resources for growth in and the practice of prayer and giving structure to a united expression of prayer by people around the world. I told Dr. Wilson Weldon, then editor of *The Upper Room*, that the fact the board was inviting *me* to assume this responsibility showed the church to be in desperate straits, since I was such a novice in this area of prayer life and its development.

This responsibility *forced* me to be even more deliberate and disciplined in my own personal life of prayer, but it introduced me to a wider dimension of spirituality than I had known. During those days, I knew no one within the Protestant tradition who was talking about *spiritual formation*. The Roman Catholics have known the importance of this aspect of Christian growth and have used "formation" language through the centuries. It wasn't long before we at The Upper Room were talking about spiritual formation and seeking to provide resources for a broader expression of spirituality than we had known before.

I became intensely interested in the great devotional classics. The Upper Room had published a collection of little booklets—selections from some of the great spiritual writings of the ages, writers whose names I barely knew, and to whose writings I was a stranger: Julian of Norwich, William Law, François Fénelon, Francis of Assisi,

Evelyn Underhill, Brother Lawrence, and an array of others. I began a deliberate practice of "keeping company with the saints," seeking to immerse myself in the writings of these folks, which have endured through the centuries, expressing Christian faith and life and becoming classic resources for the Christian pilgrim.

I am ready to confess with Leon Bloy that "there is only one sorrow, the sorrow of not being a saint." This workbook is an effort to introduce readers to the writings of four of these persons who are giants in their contribution to spiritual writing and in the role they have played in shaping spirituality: William Law, Julian of Norwich, Brother Lawrence, and Teresa of Avila. I pray that what these saints say will not only *guide and shape us*, the primary objective of this book, but will also draw us to these individuals and their writings, thus beginning a deliberate, ongoing journey of "Keeping Company with the Saints."

As I have kept company with the saints, I have observed some characteristics they have in common:

- They passionately sought the Lord.
- They discovered a gracious God.
- They took scripture seriously.
- Jesus was alive in their experience.
- They practiced discipline, at the heart of which was prayer.
- They were convinced that obedience was essential to their life and growth.
- They didn't seek ecstasy but surrender of their will to the Lord.
- They were thirsty for holiness.
- They lived not for themselves but for God and for others.
- They knew joy and peace, transcending all circumstances.

Teresa of Avila made a confession, which could be the common confession of all these saints. "The dissatisfaction we often feel when we have passed a great part of the day without being retired and absorbed in God, though we have been employed in works of obedience or charity, proceeds from a very subtle self-love, which disguises and hides itself. For it is a wish on our part to please ourselves rather than God" (*Year with the Saints*, 214). Saint Vincent de Paul expressed a similar attitude: "What a great benefit it would be to us if God would plant in our hearts a holy aversion to our own satisfaction, to which nature attaches us so strongly that we desire that others would adapt themselves to us, and all succeed well with us. Let us ask Him to teach us to place all of our happiness in Him, to love all that He loves, and to be pleased only with what pleases Him" (*Year with the Saints*, 215).

It is my prayer, as you join me in *Keeping Company with the Saints*, that the channels from our emptiness to God's fullness will be opened, that we will find inspiration and direction to live a life in which we perform faithfully what God requires of us each moment and leave the thought of everything else to him. Living in that way will bring us fulfillment, meaning, joy, purpose, and peace.

On pages 16–17 there is a brief introduction to the saints with whom we will be keeping company. You will want to read these paragraphs early in your use of the workbook.

This workbook style for Christian growth was a gift of the spirit to me. I mentioned earlier that one of the turning points in my life was joining the staff of The Upper Room to work in the area of prayer and spiritual formation. Early in my ministry there I immersed myself specifically in the literature of prayer. There is a massive resource for prayer, written by persons throughout the centuries. Perhaps more books have been written about prayer than any other single aspect of the Christian life. I discovered, in that process of vast reading, that one could read all of one's life about prayer—and never pray. I became intrigued by that phenomenon. As a result of much prayer, conversation, and reflection, I was guided to write *The Workbook of Living Prayer*. It was my desire to produce a resource on prayer that would engage a person in prayer in the very process of using the material. Thus the workbook format emerged first in *The Workbook of Living Prayer*, published in 1974. I am using that same format for this journey with the saints. I want you to read what these writers have said (sometimes translating it into your own language), reflect on the meaning of the passages, and put their messages into practice, so that you will grow in your knowledge and love of God and come "to maturity, to the measure of the full stature of Christ"(Ephesians 4:13).

Phyllis McGinley concluded the introductory chapter of her book *Saint-Watching* with this word:

> And if I cannot learn how to fly like them [the saints] or sing like them, I can learn a little of their ways. I can study the courtesy of Francis, the generosity of Bridget, the unpretentiousness of Philip, the self-command of Augustine, the kindness of Thomas, or that merriment in the face of adversity which was peculiarly Teresa's. It gives me, I repeat, an occupation, and I hope it will at length give me a little grace. (*Saint-Watching*, 12–13)

Who knows? You may be surprised by what will happen in your life as you "keep company with the saints."

THE PLAN

This workbook is designed for individual and group use. Let's look at the process. It is simple but important.

I have learned from my long years of teaching and ministry with small groups that a six- to eight-week period for a group study is the most manageable and effective. Also, people can best appropriate content and truth in "small doses." That is the reason for organizing the material in segments to be read daily.

The plan for this workbook calls for a seven-week commitment. You are asked to give about thirty minutes each day to reflect on some dimension of the Christian faith and life, suggested by one of the saints with whom you will be keeping company. For most persons, the thirty minutes will come at the beginning of the day. However, if it is not possible for you to give the time at the beginning of the day, do it whenever the time is available, but do it regularly. This is not only an intellectual pursuit; it is also a spiritual journey, the purpose of which is to incorporate the content into your daily life. This journey is personal, but my hope is that you will share it with some fellow pilgrims who will meet together once each week during the seven weeks of the study.

The workbook is arranged into seven major divisions, each designed to guide you for one week. These divisions contain seven sections, one for each day of the week. Each day of the week will have three major aspects: (1) reading, (2) reflecting and recording ideas and thoughts about the material and your own understanding and experience, (3) some practical suggestions for incorporating ideas from the reading material into your daily life.

In each day's section, you will read a selection from one of the saints and my commentary. It won't be too much to read, but it will be enough to challenge thought and action.

Quotations other than scripture are identified in parentheses at the end of each selection. The citation includes the author's name, book title, and page numbers on which the quote can be found. These citations are keyed to the Resources section at the back of the workbook. There you will find a complete bibliography should you wish to read certain works more fully.

Throughout the workbook you will see this symbol ✦ ✦ ✦. When you come to the symbol, *please stop*. Do not read any further. Think and reflect as you are requested to do in order to internalize the ideas being shared or the experience reflected upon.

REFLECTING AND RECORDING

After the reading each day, there will be a time for reflecting and recording. This dimension calls for you to record some of your reflections. The degree of meaning you receive from this workbook depends largely on your faithfulness in practicing its method. You may be unable on a particular day to do precisely what is requested. If so, then simply record that fact and make a note of why you can't follow through. This exercise may give you some insight about yourself and help you to grow.

On some days you will be asked to put in your own words the quotes from the saints. This is an important exercise. The language and style of these passages is dated. Sometimes, to really understand them, we have to paraphrase them into our everyday speech. This is a helpful exercise within itself, so I urge you to respond.

Also, on some days there may be more suggestions than you can deal with in the time you have available. Do what is most meaningful for you, and do not feel guilty about the rest.

Finally, always remember that this pilgrimage is personal. What you write in your workbook is your private property. You may not wish to share it with anyone. For this reason, no two people should attempt to share the same workbook. The importance of what you write is not what it may mean to someone else but what it means to you. Writing, even if only brief notes or single-word reminders, helps us clarify our feelings and thinking.

The significance of the reflecting-and-recording dimension will grow as you move along. Even beyond the seven weeks, you will find meaning in looking back to what you wrote on a particular day in response to a particular situation.

Sharing with Others

In the history of Christian spirituality, the spiritual director or guide has been a significant person. To varying degrees, most of us have had spiritual directors—individuals to whom we have turned for support and direction in our spiritual pilgrimage. There is a sense in which this workbook can be a spiritual guide, for you can use it as a private venture without participating in a group. Also, in a very real way, you will meet and keep company with individuals who have guided many in their spiritual journeys.

The value of the workbook will be enhanced, however, if you share the adventure with eight to twelve others. (Larger numbers tend to limit individual involvement.) In this way, you will profit from the growing insights of others, and they will profit from yours. The text includes a guide for group sharing at the end of each week.

If this is a group venture, everyone should begin their personal involvement with the workbook on the same day, so that when you come together to share as a group, all of you will have been dealing with the same material and will be at the same place in the text. It will be helpful if you have an initial get-acquainted group meeting to begin the adventure. A guide for this meeting is provided in this introduction.

Group sessions for this workbook are designed to last one and one-half hours (with the exception of the initial meeting). Those sharing in the group should covenant to attend all sessions unless an emergency prevents attendance. There will be seven weekly sessions in addition to this first get-acquainted time.

Group Leader's Task

One person may provide the leadership for the entire seven weeks, or leaders may be assigned from week to week. The leader's tasks are:

1. Read the directions and determine ahead of time how to handle the session. It may not be possible to use all the suggestions for sharing and praying together. Feel free to select those you think will be most meaningful and those for which you have adequate time.

2. Model a style of openness, honesty, and warmth. A leader does not ask anyone to share what he or she is not willing to share. Usually, as leader, be the first to share, especially as it relates to personal experiences.

3. Moderate the discussion.

4. Encourage reluctant members to participate and try to prevent a few group members from doing all the talking.

5. Keep the sharing centered in personal experience rather than academic debate.

6. Honor the time schedule. If it appears necessary to go longer than one and one-half hours, the leader should get consensus for continuing another twenty or thirty minutes.

7. See that the meeting time and place are known by all, especially if meetings are held in different homes.

8. Make sure that the necessary materials for meetings are available and that the meeting room is arranged ahead of time.

It is a good idea to hold weekly meetings in the homes of the participants. (Hosts or hostesses may make sure there are as few interruptions as possible from children, telephones, pets, and so forth.) If the meetings are held in a church, plan to be in an informal setting. Participants are asked to dress casually, to be comfortable and relaxed.

If refreshments are planned, serve them *after* the formal meeting. In this way, those who wish to stay longer for informal discussion may do so, while those who need to keep to the time schedule will be free to leave, having had the full value of the meeting time.

SUGGESTIONS FOR INITIAL GET-ACQUAINTED MEETING

Since the initial meeting is for the purpose of getting acquainted and beginning the shared pilgrimage, here is a way to get started.

1. Have each person in the group give his or her full name and the name by which each wishes to be called. Address all persons by the first name or nickname. If nametags are needed, provide them. Each group member may make a list of the names somewhere in his or her workbook.

2. Let each person in the group share one of the happiest, most exciting, or most meaningful experiences he or she has had during the past three or four weeks.

3. After this experience of happy sharing, ask each person who is willing to share his or her expectations of this workbook study to do so. Why did he or she become a part of it? What does each expect to gain from it? What are the reservations?

4. Review the introduction to the workbook and ask if there are questions about directions and procedures. (As leader, you should have read the introduction prior to the meeting.) If people have not received copies of the workbook, hand out the books now. Remember that everyone must have his or her own workbook.

5. Day One in the workbook is the day following this initial meeting, and the next meeting should be held on Day Seven of the first week. If the group must choose a weekly meeting time other than seven days from this initial session, the reading assignment may be adjusted so that the weekly meetings are always on Day Seven, and Day One is always the day following a weekly meeting.

6. Nothing binds group members together more than praying for one another. Encourage each participant to write the names of all individuals in the group in his or her workbook and commit to praying for them by name daily during the seven weeks.

7. After checking to see that everyone knows the time and place of the next meeting, close with a prayer, thanking God for each person in the group, for the opportunity for growth, and for the possibility of growing through spiritual disciplines.

BIOGRAPHIES

William Law

William Law was born in 1686 in King's Cliffe, England. He was educated at Emmanuel College, Cambridge University, graduating in 1711. He took orders in the Church of England and was appointed a fellow at Cambridge. However, he found himself unable to swear the oath of allegiance to King George I and was therefore forced to give up his orders and his university appointment.

In 1727 Law began tutoring the son of Edward Gibbon for Cambridge. The son of this boy was to become the well-known English historian who wrote *The History of the Decline and Fall of the Roman Empire*.

After completion of his tutoring of the young Gibbon boy, Law stayed with the Gibbon family for another fifteen years as spiritual advisor. During this period Law influenced many, including John and Charles Wesley. Law's *A Serious Call to a Devout and Holy Life* was highly esteemed by John Wesley, though the two did have sharp disagreements on some aspects of Law's writings. William Law died in 1761.

Teresa of Avila

Saint Teresa of Avila was born on March 28, 1515, in Spain. From an early age, she was interested in spiritual things. When just a girl, after reading of the martyrdom of the saints, she persuaded her brother to go with her to the land of the Moors. They would go as beggars for the love of God and would be beheaded for their faith. Their plan was discovered and the two were brought back. Following her failure to become a martyr for her faith, Teresa then persuaded her brother to build hermitages in their garden and pretended to be a nun, giving alms to those in need.

Her mother died when Teresa was just thirteen, and she was then raised by a stepsister. However, when that sister became caught up in her own marriage plans, Teresa was left to her own devices and found herself being drawn by the pleasures this world had to offer. She fell ill and went to stay with an uncle during her convalescence. She began reading in his library and determined that the religious life was the safest for her. Her father would not give consent, so she ran away yet again and joined the Convent of the Incarnation in Avila in 1536. Throughout her cloistered life she emphasized a life of prayer.

Feeling that her Order was becoming too lax, Teresa founded over the next twenty years a total of sixteen houses for nuns and two for friars. She died on October 4, 1582.

Julian of Norwich

Little is known of Julian's life except what she has revealed in her writings. She was apparently born somewhere around 1342, six years before the Black Death (bubonic plague) came to England. When she was around thirty years old, she suffered a severe illness, in the midst of which she had a series of visions or revelations. She spent the next twenty years pondering these visions and then writing about them, expounding on the love of God working through his mercy and grace. Her thoughts are recorded in *The Revelations of Divine Love*, the first book known to be written by a woman in English.

Because of her apparent education, it is thought that Julian must have spent a long time as a nun, as that is the only place she could have received such training. Eventually, she became an anchoress at the church of Saint Julian in Norwich, moving there sometime before 1394 and living alone in a little cell built onto the church. She may have taken her name from the male saint for whom the church was named. Julian died sometime after 1415.

Brother Lawrence

Nicholas Herman, known to us as Brother Lawrence, was born into a peasant family in Lorraine, France, in 1611. At the age of eighteen, he awakened to the presence of God in nature by gazing upon a bare tree in winter and thinking about its coming renewal. Later he became a professional soldier but was wounded and retired from the army, thereafter walking with a severe limp that troubled him throughout the rest of his life. Sometime later, he became a footman, apparently with no great success, attempted living as a hermit, which was also not successful, and then joined the Carmelite Order in Paris. He was there as a lay brother, serving in the kitchen and as a cobbler. Brother Lawrence is best known for the record of his conversations and writings entitled *The Practice of the Presence of God*. He died on February 12, 1691.

NOTE ON THE TEXTS

Quotations from William Law, Teresa of Avila, Julian of Norwich, and Brother Lawrence have not been edited for inclusive language but retain the original language, which uses male pronouns for referencing humanity and God.

The Stance
We Take

DAY
1

A Heart Wide Open to God

Robert Llewelyn titled his collection of readings from the saints throughout the year *The Joy of the Saints*. He contends that the primary secret of the joy of the saints is "a heart wide open to God and stripped of all desire for self-gratification" (xi). In his introduction to another work, he further comments:

> It is deep in our human nature to seek to justify ourselves for our conduct, and it is likely that much self-examination of conscience, however worthy the pretext we may present, is a disguised attempt to reveal that our actions were more worthy than we now fear them to be. Jean-Pierre de Caussade gives the great rule which governs the lives of the saints: "Leave the past to the infinite mercy of God, the future to his good providence; give the present wholly to his love by being faithful to his grace." (de Caussade, *Flame of Divine Love*, 4)

If we are to diligently seek, find, enjoy, and be shaped by our Creator, our stance must be to have a heart wide open to God. This was the stance of the psalmist.

> *O God, you are my God, I seek you,*
>   *my soul thirsts for you;*
> *my flesh faints for you,*
>   *as in a dry and weary land where there is no water.*
> *So I have looked upon you in the sanctuary,*
>   *beholding your power and glory.*
> *Because your steadfast love is better than life,*
>   *my lips will praise you.*
> *So I will bless you as long as I live;*
>   *I will lift up my hands and call on your name.*
>
> *My soul is satisfied as with a rich feast,*
>   *and my mouth praises you with joyful lips*
> *when I think of you on my bed,*

and meditate on you in the watches of the night;
for you have been my help,
and in the shadow of your wings I sing for joy.
My soul clings to you;
Your right hand upholds me.

—Psalm 63:1-8

William Law reminds us that a heart wide open to God is a matter of our will, obedience, and trust.

> It is the state of our will that makes the state of our life; when we receive everything from God and do everything for God, everything does us the same good and helps us to the same degree of happiness.
>
> Sickness and health, prosperity and adversity, bless and purify such a soul in the same degree; as it turns everything towards God, so everything becomes divine to it. For he that seeks God in everything is sure to find God in everything.
>
> When we thus live wholly unto God, God is wholly ours, and we are then happy in all the happiness of God. For by uniting with him in heart and will and spirit, we are united to all that he is and has in himself.
>
> This is the purity and perfection of life that we pray for in the Lord's prayer, that God's kingdom may come and his will be done in us as it is in heaven. And this we may be sure is not only necessary but attainable by us, or our Saviour would not have made it a part of our daily prayer. (*Christian Devotion*, 51)

REFLECTING AND RECORDING

Reflect on each of the following affirmations of Law's. Concentrate on each of them and write them in your own words before moving on to the next.

It is the state of our will that makes the state of our life.

As [the soul] turns everything towards God, so everything becomes divine to it. For he that seeks God in everything is sure to find God in everything.

Spend a bit of time reflecting how the following affirmation has been true in your life.

Sickness and health, prosperity and adversity, bless and purify . . . a soul in the same degree.

Close your time by praying that the adventure with this workbook will create in you the stance of a heart wide open to God.

DURING THE DAY

As you move through this day, practice *receiving* everything *from* God and *doing* everything *for* God.

DAY
2

The Boundless Abyss
of All That Is Good

Begin your time today with some reflection. How do you perceive God? Be honest and write down the first five words or phrases that express your understanding of who God is and what God is like.

1.

2.

3.

4.

5.

Praise is due to you,
  O God, in Zion;
and to you shall vows be performed,
  O you who answer prayer!
To you all flesh shall come.
When deeds of iniquity overwhelm us,
  you forgive our transgressions.
Happy are those whom you choose and bring near
  to live in your courts.
We shall be satisfied with the goodness of your house,
  your holy temple.

By awesome deeds you answer us with deliverance,
  O God of our salvation;
you are the hope of all the ends of the earth
  and of the farthest seas.
By your strength you established the mountains;
  you are girded with might.
You silence the roaring of the seas,
  the roaring of their waves,
  the tumult of the peoples.
Those who live at earth's farthest bounds are awed by your signs;
you make the gateways of the morning and the evening shout for joy.
         —Psalm 65:1-8

For God so loved the world that he gave his only Son, so that everyone who believes in him may not perish but may have eternal life.

         —John 3:16

The Lord is not slow about his promise, as some think of slowness, but is patient with you, not wanting any to perish, but all to come to repentance.

         —2 Peter 3:9

This is the message we have heard from him and proclaim to you, that God is light and in him there is no darkness at all.

         —1 John 1:5

But God, who is rich in mercy, out of the great love with which he loved us even when we were dead through our trespasses, made us alive together with Christ— by grace you have been saved—and raised us up with him and seated us with him in the heavenly places in Christ Jesus, so that in the ages to come he might show the immeasurable riches of his grace in kindness toward us in Christ Jesus. For by grace you have been saved through faith, and this is not your own doing; it is the gift of God—not the result of works, so that no one may boast. For we are what he has made us, created in Christ Jesus for good works, which God prepared beforehand to be our way of life.

—Ephesians 2:4-10

In the left column is a marvelous word from William Law about the nature of God. He says God is "nothing else but the boundless Abyss of all that is good, and sweet, and amiable." Read this passage, then read my paraphrase of it in the right column:

God, considered in Himself, is as infinitely separate from all possibility of doing hurt, or willing pain to any creature, as He is from a possibility of suffering pain or hurt from the hand of a man.

When we center our thoughts on God's nature, we realize that it is impossible for God to hurt any person. As it is beyond the possibility of any of us to bring pain or suffering to God, so it is totally beyond God's nature to will pain to any of us.

[This is] because He is in Himself, in His Holy Trinity, nothing else but the boundless Abyss of all that is good, and sweet, and amiable; and therefore stands in the utmost contrariety to every thing that is not a blessing, in an eternal impossibility of willing and intending a moment's pain or hurt to any creature.

As Father, Son, and Holy Spirit, God's goodness and love are limitless. It is like a fresh stream that will flow forever, never drying up. Therefore, it is beyond God's loving nature to will for us even a single moment of pain or hurt.

For, from this unbounded Source of goodness and perfection, nothing but infinite streams of blessing are perpetually flowing forth upon all nature and creature, in a more incessant plenty than rays of light stream from the sun.

Endless streams of love, mercy, and goodness bless us always. These streams of blessing are more present and expansive than the rays of light coming from the sun.

And as the sun has but one nature and can give forth nothing but the blessings of light, so the Holy Triune God has but one nature and intent towards all the creation, which is, to pour forth the riches and sweetness of his divine perfections upon every thing that is capable of them and according to its capacity to receive them. (*Wholly for God*, 118–19)

As the sun can only send forth the blessings of light, so the Triune God—the Father, Son, and Holy Spirit—has a singular intention: to pour forth the riches of divine perfection upon us. We will receive these blessings according to our openness to God's grace and our capacity to be receptive.

Persons of every age have sought to describe this core characteristic of God's nature. Isaac of Syria, in the seventh century, described God as "that spring of love whose supply never fails" (*Joy of the Saints*, 8). George Beverly Shea, song leader for the Billy Graham Crusades, made popular a gospel song seeking to portray the expansiveness of God's love:

> The love of God is greater far than tongue or pen can ever tell;
> It goes beyond the highest star, and reaches to the lowest hell;
> The guilty pair, bowed down with care, God gave His Son to win;
> His erring child He reconciled, and pardoned from his sin.
>
> When years of time shall pass away, and earthly thrones and kingdoms fall,
> When men, who here refuse to pray, on rocks and hills and mountains call,
> God's love so sure shall still endure, all measureless and strong;
> Redeeming grace to Adam's race—the saints' and angels' song.
>
> Could we with ink the ocean fill, and were the skies of parchment made,
> Were every stalk on earth a quill, and every man a scribe by trade,
> To write the love of God above would drain the ocean dry;
> Nor could the scroll contain the whole, though stretched from sky to sky.
>
> Refrain:
> O love of God, how rich and pure!
> How measureless and strong!
> It shall forevermore endure
> The saints' and angels' song!

Text: Frederick M. Lehman
Based on the Jewish poem "Hadamut," by Meir Ben Isaac Nehorai

REFLECTING AND RECORDING

Go back to your beginning reflection about God's nature. How does your expression harmonize with the above scripture passages, Law's understanding, Isaac of

Syria, and the gospel hymn? How are you challenged to rethink your understanding of God?

✤   ✤   ✤

DURING THE DAY

The following affirmations are printed at the back of the book:

> God is "the boundless Abyss of all that is good, and sweet, and amiable."
>
> —William Law

> God alone is that spring of love whose supply never fails.
>
> —Isaac of Syria

Cut these out and carry them with you, reading them as often as possible. Do this until you have memorized them and can carry them always in your heart. Continue the discipline by receiving everything from God and doing everything for God.

DAY
3

All That He Has Done
He Has Done for Me Alone

Yesterday we considered William Law's contention that God is "nothing else but the boundless Abyss of all that is good, and sweet, and amiable." God's love and goodness are limitless. It is beyond God's will and nature to will for us even a single moment of pain or hurt.

Today we continue to meditate on that claim by considering the testimony of Julian of Norwich:

> My bodily eyes I fixed on the same cross (on which I had gazed for my comfort before this time): my tongue I occupied with speech of Christ's passion and with rehearsing the faith of Holy Church: and my heart I

fastened on God with all my trust and might. *(Revelations of Divine Love,* 182*)*

It is God's will that I see myself as much bound to him in love, as if all that he hath done he had done for me. And thus should every soul think in regard of his Lover. *(Revelations of Divine Love,* 174–75*)*

And it is his will that our hearts be mightily raised above the depths of the earth and all vain sorrows, and rejoice in him. *(Revelations of Divine Love,* 180*)*

For he loveth us and liketh us; and so willeth he that we love him and like him, and mightily trust in him. And all shall be well. *(Revelations of Divine Love,* 181*)*

Focus on that fantastic claim: "It is God's will that I see myself as much bound to him in love, as if all that he hath done he had done for me." The most dramatic demonstration of God's love is the cross, so Julian confesses, "My bodily eyes I fixed on the cross." Paul put it succinctly: "Live in love, as Christ loved us and gave himself for us, a fragrant offering and sacrifice to God" (Eph. 5:2).

One of the clearest and most challenging descriptions of Christ in the Bible is in Paul's Letter to the Philippians:

Let the same mind be in you that was in Christ Jesus, who, though he was in the form of God, did not regard equality with God as something to be exploited, but emptied himself, taking the form of a slave, being born in human likeness. And being found in human form, he humbled himself and became obedient to the point of death—even death on a cross.

—Philippians 2:5-8, NKJV

There's a wonderful story from Sweden about the cross and its place in our life. Back in 1716, King Charles XII announced to a little town that he was going to come and visit and that he would worship in the village church. The pastor of the church got all excited about the presence of the king in his congregation. He decided to put aside the prescribed text for that Sunday and to deliver a sermon in the form of a eulogy on the greatness of the royal family. He did that.

Three months later a gift from the king arrived at the church; it was in a big box. The pastor was thrilled. But he wasn't ready for that particular present. Inside the box he found a life-sized crucifix, a statue of Jesus on the cross, with this instruction: "Place this on the pillar opposite the pulpit, so that the one who stands in the pulpit to preach will always be reminded of his proper subject."

Not only a preacher needs to keep eyes on the crucified Lord in order to maintain the "proper subject for preaching"; all of us need to keep our heart's eye on the cross in order to stay aware of how much God loves us. It is for "the world" that God gave God's only begotten Son (John 3:16). Our secret for confidence in our relationship to God is to see the cross "as if all that he hath done he had done for me."

REFLECTING AND RECORDING:

Julian says, "It is God's will that I see myself as much bound to him in love." To what degree do you see yourself bound to God in love? Write a paragraph answering this question. Probe deeply and respond honestly.

Recall and describe a time or an experience in your life when you felt that Jesus' death on the cross was for you.

Pray this prayer as you close your time of reflecting and recording:

> O love that wilt not let me go,
> I rest my weary soul in thee;
> I give thee back the life I owe,
> that in thine ocean depths its flow may richer, fuller be. (George Matheson)

DURING THE DAY

Continue reading the affirmations you cut out yesterday. Also continue your discipline of *receiving* everything *from* God and *doing* everything *for* God.

DAY
4

Love Was Our Lord's Meaning

Beloved, let us love one another, for love is of God; everyone who loves is born of God and knows God. Whoever does not love does not know God, for God is love. God's love was revealed among us in this way: God sent his only Son into the world so that we might live through him. In this is love, not that we loved God, but that he loved us and sent his Son to be the atoning sacrifice for our sins. Beloved, since God loved us so much, we also ought to love one another. No one has ever seen God; if we love one another, God lives in us, and his love is perfected in us.

—1 John 4:7-12

From the time that it was revealed, I often desired to know what our Lord's meaning was. After more than fifteen years, I was answered in spiritual understanding, "What? Would you know your Lord's meaning in this thing? Know it well: love was the meaning. Who showed it to you? Love. What did God show you? Love. Why did God show it? For love. Hold on to that, and you will understand more of the same. But apart from that, you will never understand anything."

So I was taught that love is our Lord's meaning. I saw more surely in this and in all that our God made that God loved us, and this love never was satisfied and never will be. All God's works have been done in this love, and in this love God has made everything that is for our benefit, and in this love our life is everlasting. In our creation, we had a beginning, but the love in which God made us was in God without beginning. In this love we have our beginning. (*Encounter with God's Love*, 65–66)

When will we learn it? Love was our Lord's meaning. Knowing this changes our lives and our relationships.

Most of us are familiar with the concept of self-fulfilling prophecy. The theory contends that we conform to the image we have of ourselves. If we see ourselves as intelligent, we will act intelligently. If we see ourselves as inferior, unacceptable, unlovable, unworthy, that is how we will behave. If we see ourselves as a klutz or clumsy, we will perform in that fashion.

A marvelous illustration of this, in Ron Lee Davis's book *Mistreated*, is a tale of two altar boys. One was born in 1892 in Eastern Europe. The other boy was born just three years later in a small town in Illinois. These two altar boys had almost identical experiences, though they lived in different parts of the world. Each boy was given the opportunity to assist his parish priest in the service of Holy Communion. Not surprisingly, each boy, while handling the Communion cup, once actually spilled some of the wine on the carpet. But there the kinship with each other ended.

Seeing the purple stain on the carpet, the priest of the Eastern European church slapped the altar boy across the face, saying, "Clumsy oaf! Leave the altar!" That little boy grew up to become an atheist and a communist. His name was Josip Bronz Tito, the dictator of Yugoslavia from 1943–80.

The priest in the church in Illinois responded in a completely different way. Seeing the stain near the altar, he knelt down to the level of the little boy and said, "It is all right, son. You will do better next time. You will be a fine priest of God someday." That little boy grew up to become the much beloved Bishop Fulton J. Sheen (*Mistreated*, 138–39).

As I have lived with scripture for over forty years now, I have not discovered a single place in scripture where God's love is dependent upon something we *do*. There is no time when God says, "If . . . , then I will love you." There are countless examples of God's promise to act being dependent upon conditions we must meet. A classic example in the Hebrew Bible is found in 2 Chronicles 7:14: "If my people who are called by my name will humble themselves, pray, seek my face, and turn from their wicked ways, then I will hear from heaven, and will forgive their sin and heal their land." The classic example in the New Testament is Jesus' promise to abide in us if we abide in him. He is explicit:

If you abide in me, and my words abide in you, ask whatever you wish, and it shall be done for you. . . . If you keep my commandments, you will abide in my love, just as I have kept my Father's commandments and abide in his love.

—John 15:7, 10

But never is God's *love* dependent upon some condition we are to meet. God loves us, period. Nothing added. No limiting definitions.

Countless folks have discovered with Julian that "love is our Lord's meaning." Nothing has more potential for transforming our lives and relationships than that understanding.

REFLECTING AND RECORDING

Spend a minute or two reflecting on each of Julian's following claims.

In all that our God made . . . God loved us.

✤ ✤ ✤

This love never was satisfied and never will be.

✤ ✤ ✤

In this love God has made everything that is for our benefit.

✤ ✤ ✤

In this love our life is everlasting.

✤ ✤ ✤

Now put into your own words in the space below this paragraph by Julian:

So I was taught that love is our Lord's meaning. I saw more surely in this and in all that our God made that God loved us, and this love never was satisfied and never will be. All God's works have been done in this love, and in this love God has made everything that is for our benefit, and in this love our life is everlasting. In our creation, we had a beginning, but the love in which God made us was in God without beginning. In this love we have our beginning.

DURING THE DAY

Continue reading the affirmations you cut out on Day Two. Also, continue your discipline of *receiving* everything *from* God and *doing* everything *for* God.

DAY
5

Our Courteous Lord

There was a man who had two sons. The younger of them said to his father, "Father, give me the share of the property that will belong to me." So he divided his property between them. A few days later the younger son gathered all he had and traveled to a distant country, and there he squandered his property in dissolute living. When he had spent everything, a severe famine took place throughout that country, and he began to be in need. So he went and hired himself out to one of the citizens of that country, who sent him to his fields to feed the pigs. He would gladly have filled himself with the pods that the pigs were eating; and no one gave him anything. But when he came to himself he said, "how many of my father's hired hands have bread enough and to spare, but here I am dying of hunger! I will get up and go to my father, and I will say to him, "Father, I have sinned against heaven and before you; I am no longer worthy to be called your son; treat me like one of your hired hands." So he set off and went to his father. But while he was still far off, his father saw him and was filled with compassion; he ran and put his arms around him and kissed him. Then the son said to him, "Father, I have sinned against heaven and before you; I am no longer worthy to be called your son." But the father said to his slaves, "Quickly, bring out a robe—the best one— and put it on him; put a ring on his finger and sandals on his feet. And get the fatted calf and kill it, and let us eat and celebrate; for this son of mine was dead and is alive again; he was lost and is found!" And they began to celebrate.

—Luke 15:11-24

God's love is greater than our sin. God's willingness to forgive is the open door to new life, which includes freedom from sin and guilt. Sin does not, *cannot* prevent God from loving us. Julian of Norwich says:

Our good Lord protects us most preciously when it seems to us that we are nearly forsaken and cast away for our sin because we see that we have deserved it.

[O]ur courteous Lord does not want his servants to despair over falling often or falling deeply. Our falling does not prevent him from loving us. . . .

This is the sovereign friendship of our courteous Lord, who protects us so tenderly while we are in our sin. Furthermore, he touches us most secretly and shows us our sin by the sweet light of mercy and grace. . . .

Our courteous Lord shows himself to the soul simply and full of glad cheer, as if the soul had been in pain and in prison, saying, "My dear darling, I am glad you have come to me in all your sorrow. I have always been with you." (*Encounter with God's Love*, 37–38)

A preacher friend recently shared with me the story of his prodigal son's return from the far country. The son was thirty-three years old. He had become addicted first to marijuana at age sixteen. This led to the dark, miserable, dangerous depths of almost every kind of drug use. Months would go by without any contact with the family. There were stints in jail, bouts of homelessness on the streets, periods in treatment centers, almost-fatal accidents. He would bear the marks of his sojourn in the far country forever.

The son was drawn from the "pigpen" of his tortured life by the memory of his parents' love and the gospel message his father preached: "God loves you as though you were the only person in the world to love." He tested it out in a Christian community for recovering addicts. Without letting his parents know, he participated in a treatment program for three months—a program centered in God's love, including honesty, confession, repentance, accountability, and reimagining the future with Christ at the center. He stayed around the community for three more months.

The parents had not heard from the son for nine months. Their last news was that he was living on the streets in Phoenix. Only a week before the father shared this story with me, his son had called. No contact for nine months and now this word: "I've found Christ and I've found myself. I'm coming home. What you have preached about God's love is true." You can imagine the celebration that had gone on that week.

REFLECTING AND RECORDING

Next week we'll look more at sin and temptation. For now, spend a few minutes thinking about Jesus as *our courteous Lord*. Do you believe that "our falling does not prevent him from loving us"? Wrestle with this for a few minutes. Be honest.

✦ ✦ ✦

Who in your family or among your friends is in "the far country," not aware of or accepting the love of Christ? Name that person here.

Do you believe that individual's lifestyle or failings prevent our Lord from loving him or her? Pray for that person now.

✤   ✤   ✤

Recall a personal experience when Christ has shown you your sin "by the sweet light of mercy and grace." Record that experience briefly here.

DURING THE DAY

When anything calls you to prayer today, remember your friend in the "far country" and pray for that person.

Continue reading the affirmations you cut out on Day Two.

DAY
6

"The Overflowing Fountain of Good"

Yesterday we considered the fact that God's love is greater than our sin. But there is even more. William Law referred to God's love as an overflowing fountain of good that sends forth nothing but good for all eternity.

> [God] is the Good, the unchangeable, overflowing Fountain of good, that sends forth nothing but good to all eternity. He is the Love itself, the unmixed, unmeasurable Love, doing nothing but from love, giving nothing but gifts of love, to every thing that He has made; requiring nothing of all His creatures, but the spirit and fruits of that love, which brought them into being.
>
> Oh, how sweet is this contemplation of the height and depth of the riches of divine Love! With what attraction must it draw every thoughtful man to return love for love to this overflowing Fountain of boundless goodness!
>
> View every part of our redemption, from Adam's first sin, to the resurrection of the dead, and you will find nothing but successive mysteries of that first love which created angels and men. All the mysteries of the gospel are only so many marks and proofs of God's desiring to make His Love triumph, in the removal of sin and disorder from all nature and creature. (*Wholly for God*, 119–20)

My friend Grace Marie Prince died on January 27, 1999, at the age of ninety-four. She was a vibrant witness of love's triumph. At nineteen, she married a Methodist preacher, who died three years later from a brain tumor. Grace's only child was born one month after this untimely death. Life taught Grace to pray. Instead of being crushed by a life of hardships, she returned "love for love to this overflowing Fountain of boundless goodness."

Two of Grace's three grandchildren are United Methodist ministers. One of them, Karla Kincannon, gave a tribute at the funeral service, concluding with this challenging testimony:

Nana loved people and she loved life. She loved to sing. She sang in the church choir, sang karaoke at my wedding rehearsal dinner, and sang hymns the day before she died—just as John Wesley sang hymns right before his death.

The last eight years of her life were really hard for all of us—especially for her as she angrily slipped into senility. Only near the end did her anger subside when she could no longer remember what she was angry about. My parents, who cared for her during these eight years, have been elevated to sainthood because of their compassion and patience. It was difficult watching such a loving person lose her ability to relate to life fully. Watching her world grow increasingly narrow and small when the entire world had been her parish only a few years before was very difficult.

Sometimes the final healing comes in death. A friend of the family had a dream about Nana a few weeks ago. She dreamed she had been invited to Nana's birthday party. Expecting Nana to be sick and unable to recognize her, she went to the house. To her great surprise and delight, she was greeted by a sprightly, loving Nana who called her by name. Nana took her hands and said, "Oh, honey, it's so good to see you!" just like she used to do years before. In her dream, Nana was her true self, her very best self. The self she used to be. My friend said to me, "When Nana dies, it will be like her birthday, a rebirthing, and she will finally be herself again."

When Nana died on Wednesday night, it was like a rebirthing. In Grace's last moments, with favorite hymns playing quietly on the tape player, my mother talked to her about God's love, reminding her she could trust God's love, even in death. As Nana's breathing became labored, Mother coached her, much like a birthing coach, encouraging her to let go into God's love. Peacefully, Grace slipped from this life into the loving arms of God. And at the very moment of her last breath, the hymn "Amazing Grace" came on the tape player and those of us present sang Nana into her new life.

When the youngest member of our family was told about Nana's death, she said, "Nana won't have any more birthdays." That's right. She won't have any more birthdays because she has been birthed into eternity. In this last birthday, in her death, she has been transformed into her very best self. Thanks be to God for such amazing grace!

Grace's story is repeated over and over again in those who accept God's redemptive love. "All the mysteries of the gospel are only so many marks and proofs of God's desiring to make his love triumph." Paul summarized this movement of God's love to us in his salutation to Titus:

Paul, a servant of God and an apostle of Jesus Christ, for the sake of the faith of God's elect and the knowledge of the truth that is in accordance with godliness, in

*the hope of eternal life that God, who never lies, promised before the ages began—
in due time he revealed his word through the proclamation with which I have been
entrusted by the command of God our Savior, To Titus, my loyal child in the faith
we share: Grace and peace from God the Father and Christ Jesus our Savior.*

—Titus 1:1-4

REFLECTING AND RECORDING

Spend time reflecting on each of Law's following assertions about God's expansive love.

   . . .doing nothing but from love

✠   ✠   ✠

   . . .giving nothing but gifts of love, to every thing he has made

✠   ✠   ✠

   . . . requiring nothing of all His creatures, but the spirit and fruits of that
love, which brought them into being

✠   ✠   ✠

DURING THE DAY

Move through this day asking to do nothing but from love, give nothing but gifts of
love, and require nothing from others but that which is loving.

DAY
7

A Continuous Seeking

*As a deer longs for flowing streams,
   so my soul longs for you, O God.
My soul thirsts for God,
   for the living God.*

When shall I come and behold
the face of God?
My tears have been my food
day and night,
while people say to me continually, "Where is your God?"

These things I remember,
    as I pour out my soul:
how I went with the throng,
    and led them in procession to the house of God,
with glad shouts and songs of thanksgiving,
    a multitude keeping festival.
Why are you cast down, O my soul,
    and why are you disquieted within me?
Hope in God; for I shall again praise him
                                            —Psalm 42:1-5

For God alone my soul waits in silence;
    from him comes my salvation.
He alone is my rock and my salvation,
    my fortress; I shall never be shaken.
                                            —Psalm 62:1-2

A few months ago I was going through a dry time in my life. Outwardly things were going well. All my children seemed to be at a good place in their lives. My wife, Jerry, and I were in excellent health and were enjoying each other and our "stage" in life. Asbury Theological Seminary, where I serve as president, was thriving. We had our largest enrollment ever. The spiritual vitality of the students was inspiring. Our trustees had made the decision to establish an extension campus in Florida. I should have been "on top."

But not so. I came dragging to my morning time of scripture and devotional reading and prayer. I felt like the psalmist: "My soul thirsts for you; my flesh faints for you, as in a dry and weary land where there is no water" (Ps. 63:1). I could have prayed with the psalmist:

Why, O Lord, do you stand far off? (Ps. 10:1)

Will you forget me forever? . . . Give light to my eyes, or I will sleep the sleep of death. (Ps. 13:1-3)

My eyes grow dim with waiting for my God. (Ps. 69:3)

Concentrating during my time of devotion and prayer was difficult. I would realize that I had read a passage of scripture and not know what I had read. Or my mind would leap about as I sought to pray for a person or about a particular issue. During this time I came across the following from Julian of Norwich:

> And this vision taught me to understand that the soul's constant search pleases God greatly. For it cannot do more than seek, suffer and trust. And this is accomplished in every soul, to whom it is given by the Holy Spirit. And illumination by finding is of the Spirit's special grace, when it is his will. Seeking with faith, hope and love pleases our Lord, and finding pleases the soul and fills it full of joy. And so I was taught to understand that seeking is as good as contemplating, during the time that he wishes to permit the soul to be in labour. It is God's will that we seek on until we see him, for it is through this that he will show himself to us, of his special grace, when it is his will.
>
> And he will teach a soul himself how it should bear itself when it contemplates him, and that is the greatest honour to him and the greatest profit to the soul, and it receives most humility and other virtues, by the grace and guidance of the Holy Spirit. For it seems to me that the greatest honour which a soul can pay to God is simply to surrender itself to him with true confidence, whether it be seeking or contemplating. . . . Seeking is common to all, and every soul can have through grace and ought to have discretion and teaching from Holy Church.
>
> It is God's will that we receive three things from him as gifts as we seek. The first is that we seek willingly and diligently without sloth, as that may be with his grace, joyfully and happily, without unreasonable depression and useless sorrow. The second is that we wait for him steadfastly, out of love for him, without grumbling and contending against him, to the end of our lives, for that will last only for a time. The third is that we have great trust in him, out of complete and true faith, for it is his will that we know that he will appear, suddenly and blessedly, to all his lovers. For he works in secret, and he will be perceived, and his appearing will be very sudden. And he wants to be trusted, for he is very accessible, familiar and courteous, blessed may he be. (*Showings*, 195–96)

This passage reminded me that I was seeking the Lord, but I was not *trusting him completely*. Over a period of about three weeks I worked on my trust. I went back to my initial Christian commitment when I accepted Christ as my savior and was baptized. I rehearsed some of those trying, testing, and troubling times when I had trusted the Lord and was delivered. Gradually the confidence and the emotional experience of Christ's presence returned.

REFLECTING AND RECORDING

Our stance in relation to God is a continuous seeking. Reflect on your seeking. How do you measure up to Julian's three characteristics of seeking? Spend some time in self-examination.

Do you seek "willingly and diligently, without sloth"? "without unreasonable depression and useless sorrow"?

Do you "wait for him steadfastly . . . without grumbling and contending against him"?

Do you have "great trust in him, out of complete and true faith"?

DURING THE DAY

Continue your effort to do nothing but from love, give nothing but gifts of love, and require nothing from others but that which is loving.

Group Meeting
for Week One

INTRODUCTION

Group sessions will be most meaningful when they reflect the experience of all the participants. This guide is designed simply to facilitate personal sharing. Therefore, you need not be rigid in following these suggestions. The leader, especially, should be sensitive to what is going on in the lives of the participants and can focus the group's sharing of those experiences. Ideas are important. We need to wrestle with new ideas as well as with ideas with which we disagree. It is important, however, that the group meeting not become a debate about ideas. Put the emphasis on individuals—experiences, feelings, and meaning. Content is important, but applying content to our individual lives, our relationship to God and others, is most important.

As the group comes to the place where all can share honestly and openly what is happening in their lives, the more meaningful the experience will be. This does not mean sharing only the good or positive; share also the struggles, the difficulties, and the negatives.

This process is not easy; it is deceptive to pretend it is. Saint Francis de Sales expressed it clearly:

> **Observe that perfection is not acquired by sitting with our arms folded, but it is necessary to work in earnest, in order to conquer ourselves and to bring ourselves to live, not according to our inclinations and passions, but according to reason, our Rule, and obedience. The thing is hard, it cannot be denied, but necessary. With practice, however, it becomes easy and pleasing.** (*Year with the Saints*, 10)

Growth requires effort. Don't be afraid to share your questions, reservations, and "dry periods," as well as that in which you find meaning.

SHARING TOGETHER

1. Begin your time together by allowing each person in the group to share his or her most meaningful day with the workbook this week. The leader begins this sharing. Tell why that particular day was so meaningful.
2. Now let everyone share their most difficult day. Tell about experiences and why that day was so difficult.
3. Turn to the Reflecting and Recording section of Day One. Invite those who wish to share to tell how they rewrote the affirmations of Law.
4. Invite two people to share to what degree they see themselves *bound to God in love* (Reflecting and Recording, Day Three).
5. Invite two group members to describe a time in their life when they felt that Jesus' death on the cross was for them alone (Reflecting and Recording, Day Three).
6. Invite two or three individuals to share their "translation" of Julian (Reflecting and Recording, Day Four).
7. In light of your discussion thus far, spend six to ten minutes discussing the claim: "our failing does not hinder (God) from loving us."
8. Are there persons in the group willing to share an occasion when Christ showed them their sin "by the kindly light of mercy and grace"? (Reflecting and Recording, Day Five)
9. Invite someone to read Julian's word about the role of *trust* in our seeking (Day Seven)

Spend the balance of your time discussing and sharing personal experiences of trust, referring to the three things God wills in our seeking, according to Julian.

PRAYING TOGETHER

Each week the group is asked to pray together. Corporate prayer is one of the great blessings of Christian community. There is power in corporate prayer, and it is important to include it in our shared pilgrimage.

It is also important for everyone to feel comfortable during corporate prayer. No one should feel pressured to pray aloud. Silent corporate prayer may be as vital and meaningful as verbal corporate prayer. God does not need to hear our words spoken aloud to hear our prayers. Silence, where thinking is centered and attention is focused, may provide our deepest periods of prayer.

Verbalizing thoughts and feelings to God in the presence of fellow pilgrims can be a powerful experience for a community on a common journey too. Verbal prayers may be offered spontaneously as persons choose to pray aloud. Do not suggest, "Let's go around the circle now, and each one pray."

Suggestions for this "praying together" time will be given each week. The leader for the week should regard these only as suggestions. What is happening in the meeting—the mood, the needs that are expressed, the timing—determines the direction of the group's prayer time together. Here are some possibilities for this closing period.

1. Invite the group to spend a few minutes in silence, deliberately thinking about each person in the group, what that individual has shared, and offering a silent sentence prayer of petition or thanksgiving for that person.

2. Invite any two or three people to offer a spontaneous brief verbal prayer, thanking God for the group and the opportunity to share with others in this study/learning/prayer experience.

3. Using an instant-developing camera, take a picture of each group member. Turn pictures facedown on a table and let everyone pick up one. Each group member will pray for the person in the picture selected during the coming week. Have everyone take a few minutes to visit with the person whose picture he or she has selected. Inquire about concerns or events that could be incorporated in prayer.

Another option is for everyone to write the name of each member of the group in the front of their workbook. Everyone will pray for group members each week. By praying for one another we respond to Saint Vincent de Paul's teaching:

When we have to speak to others on spiritual matters, we ought first to speak of them to God in prayer, and empty ourselves of our own spirit, that we may be filled with the Holy Spirit, which alone illuminates the mind and inflames the will. (*Year with the Saints*, 256)

Sin and Temptation

DAY
1

The Way of the Returning Prodigal

Go back to Day Five of last week and reread the story of the prodigal son.

✦   ✦   ✦

William Law reminds us that one of his contemporaries, Jacob Behman, a spiritual writer (also known as Jacob Boehme), called his readers to be *in the way of the returning prodigal*. Commenting on this notion, Law wrote:

> It is not rules of morality observed, or an outward blameless form of life that will do: for pride, vanity, envy, self-love and love of the world can be and often are the heart of such a morality of life. But the state of the lost son is quite another thing.
>
> As soon as he comes to himself and has seeing eyes, he will then, like him, see himself far from home; that he has lost his first paradise, his heavenly Father, and the dignity of his first birth; that he is a poor, beggarly slave in a foreign land, hungry, ragged, and starving among the lowest kind of beasts, not so well fed and clothed as they are.
>
> Wherever the gospel itself is received and professed without something of this preparation of heart, without this sensibility of the lost son, there it can only be a stone of stumbling and help the earthly man to form a religion of notions and opinions from the unfelt meaning of the letter of the gospel. (*Joy of the Saints*, 298)

Our preparation of heart to receive the gospel is the way of the prodigal son. We must "come to ourselves" by being aware

- of our sin,
- that we are lost, separated from heritage and home,
- that we have violated our personhood and destiny,

- that the result of our pride and self-will is hunger, ragged clothing, and identification with the pigs.

The way home is not a rigid morality and blameless life. It is an awareness that we have lost our "first paradise" and that our Father is waiting to welcome us home. Read the balance of Jesus' parable:

> *Now his elder son was in the field; and when he came and approached the house, he heard music and dancing. He called one of the slaves and asked what was going on. He replied, "Your brother has come, and your father has killed the fatted calf, because he has got him back safe and sound." Then he became angry and refused to go in. His father came out and began to plead with him. But he answered his father, "Listen! For all these years I have been working like a slave for you, and I have never disobeyed your command; yet you have never given me even a young goat so that I might celebrate with my friends. But when this son of yours came back, who has devoured your property with prostitutes, you killed the fatted calf for him!" Then the father said to him, "Son, you are always with me and all that is mine is yours. But we had to celebrate and rejoice, because this brother of yours was dead and has come to life; he was lost and has been found."*

> —Luke 15:25-32

REFLECTING AND RECORDING

The elder brother was a good moral person, outwardly blameless, but look at him. How is his *pride* expressed?

❖   ❖   ❖

"You have never given me even a young goat so that I might celebrate with my friends." Is this vanity?

❖   ❖   ❖

"He became angry and refused to go in." Is this self-love?

❖   ❖   ❖

Would you put yourself in the place of the prodigal son or the elder brother?

❖   ❖   ❖

Whether the prodigal or the elder brother, we can be in the way of the returning prodigal. Write a prayer expressing your commitment to being in this way.

DURING THE DAY

Stanza two of the hymn "I Want a Principle Within" is printed on page 203. Cut it out and take it with you this week. Put it in your pocket or purse, on your refrigerator door or the dashboard of your car. Make it a prayer that you offer to the Lord many times each day this week.

DAY
2

Allow Your Inward Deformity To Show Itself

For we know that the law is spiritual; but I am of the flesh, sold into slavery under sin. I do not understand my own actions. For I do not do what I want, but I do the very thing I hate. Now if I do what I do not want, I agree that the law is good. But in fact it is no longer I that do it, but sin that dwells within me. For I know that nothing good dwells within me, that is, in my flesh. I can will what is right, but I cannot do it.

—Romans 7:14-18

So far as we, by true resignation to God, die to the Element of Selfishness and our own Will, so far as by universal Love, we die to the Element of Envy, so far as by Humility we die to the Element of Pride, so far as by Meekness we die to the Element of Wrath, so far we get away from the Devil, enter into another Kingdom, and leave him to dwell without us in his own Elements.

The greatest Good that any Man can do to himself, is to give lease to this inward Deformity to show itself, and not to strive by any Art or management, either of Negligence or Amusement, to conceal it from him.

First, because the Root of a dark Fire-life within us, which is of the Nature of Hell, with all its Elements of Selfishness, Envy, Pride and

Wrath, must be in some sort discovered to us, and felt by us, before we can enough feel, and enough groan under the Weight of our Disorder.

Repentance is but a kind of Table-talk till we see so much of the deformity of our inward Nature, as to be in some degree frighted and terrified at the sight of it.

There must be some kind of Earthquake within us, something that must rend and shake us to the bottom, before we can be enough sensible either of the State of Death we are in, or enough desirous of that Saviour, who alone can raise us from it. (Law, *Works*, 37–38)

In the parable of the prodigal son, Jesus said the young man "came to himself." It was only then—when he recognized that he was a poor slave in a foreign land, ragged and starving—that he made the decision to return to his father's house.

I'm sure that decision was no easy one. The young man had chosen deliberately to leave his father and come to this far country. It was an act of self-will, a desire to go it alone, to have his "inheritance" and use it as he pleased, satisfying his own desires.

Paul gave dramatic expression to the struggle that goes on within us all. "For I do not do the good I want, but the evil I do not want is what I do. Now if I do what I do not want, it is no longer I that do it, but sin that dwells within me" (Rom. 7:19-20). William Law contends that "the greatest Good that any Man can do to himself, is to give lease to this inward Deformity to show itself." Until we acknowledge our "inward deformity"—sin—there is no salvation, no healing. "Wretched man that I am!" Paul moaned (Rom. 7:24). Repentance is necessary if we are going to receive God's forgiving grace. We never repent until we are confronted by our sin. Law makes it clear. Read again Law's words in paragraphs two, three, and four above.

REFLECTING AND RECORDING

Can you recall an experience when you felt most like the prodigal son? when you *came to yourself*, realizing you were *lost*, that your *sinful self* was in control, and that you needed to return to the Father? Describe that experience here.

Read again the last paragraph from the selections by Law at the opening of this Day. Spend a few minutes pondering *if* and *how* this truth has worked in your experience.

✤ ✤ ✤

DURING THE DAY

Continue to use stanza two of "I Want a Principle Within" as a prayer throughout the day.

DAY
3

In the Jaws of Death and Hell

Imagine that you and I are friends. I have known you long enough to know your lifestyle, your inner thoughts, your dreams and passions. We have shared questions and longings, hopes and doubts. I care enough about you to be honest. One day, we are taking a long walk together. Walks together have become the occasions when we share deeply with each other. You sense that I am uneasy. I'm finding conversation difficult. You sense I want to say something but can't. Finally I screw up my courage and almost blurt out, "You are my friend, and I care so much for you. You are lying in the jaws of death and hell."

How would you respond? Write the first three thoughts you would have or responses you would make to my assessment, "You are *lying in the jaws of death and hell*."

1.

2.

3.

It's a shocking thought—being in the jaws of death and hell. It sometimes takes dramatic language and images to force us to face reality. Paul pulled no punches. "All have sinned and fall short of the glory of God" (Rom. 3:23). "All . . . are under the power of sin" (Rom. 3:9). "The wages of sin is death" (Rom. 6:23). "It was sin, working death in me" (Rom. 7:13).

All the saints and great spiritual writers gave honest attention to the plight of sin, common to us all. William Law expressed it in this fashion:

> The reason why we know so little of Jesus Christ as our Saviour, . . . why we are so destitute of that faith in him which alone can change, rectify, and redeem our souls, why we live starving in the coldness and deadness of a formal, historical, hearsay religion, is this; we are strangers to our inward misery and wants, we know not that we lie in the jaws of death and hell;

> we keep all things quiet within us partly by outward forms and modes or religion and morality, and partly by the comforts, cares, and delights of this world. Hence it is that we . . . believe in a Saviour, not because we feel an absolute want of one, but because we have been told there is one, and that it would be a rebellion against God to reject him. . . .

> True faith is a coming to Jesus Christ to be saved and delivered from a sinful nature, as the Canaanitish woman came to him and would not be denied. It is a faith . . . that in love and longing and hunger and thirst and full assurance will lay hold on Christ as its loving, assured, certain and infallible Saviour. . . .

> It is this faith that breaks off all the bars and chains of death and hell in the soul; it is to this faith that Christ always says what he said in the Gospel: "Thy faith hath saved thee, thy sins are forgiven thee; go in peace." (*Christian Devotion*, 135)

Look now at the story of the woman coming to Christ "to be saved and delivered from a sinful nature."

> *One of the Pharisees asked Jesus to eat with him, and he went into the Pharisee's house and took his place at the table. And a woman in the city, who was a sinner, having learned that he was eating in the Pharisee's house, brought an alabaster jar of ointment. She stood behind him at his feet, weeping, and began to bathe his feet with her tears and to dry them with her hair. Then she continued kissing his feet and anointing them with the ointment. Now when the Pharisee who had invited him saw it, he said to himself, "If this man were a prophet, he would have known who and what kind of woman this is who is touching him—that she is a sinner."*

*Jesus spoke up and said to him, "Simon, I have something to say to you."
"Teacher," he replied, "speak." "A certain creditor had two debtors; one owed five
hundred denarii, and the other fifty. When they could not pay, he canceled the
debts for both of them. Now which of them will love him more?" Simon
answered, "I suppose the one for whom he canceled the greater debt." And Jesus
said to him, "You have judged rightly." Then turning toward the woman, he said
to Simon, "Do you see this woman? I entered your house; you gave me no water
for my feet, but she has bathed my feet with her tears and dried them with her
hair. You gave me no kiss, but from the time I came in she has not stopped kissing
my feet. You did not anoint my head with oil, but she has anointed my feet with
ointment. Therefore, I tell you, her sins, which were many, have been forgiven;
hence she has shown great love. But the one to whom little is forgiven, loves little." Then he said to her, "Your sins are forgiven." But those who were at the table
with him began to say among themselves, "Who is this who even forgives sins?"
And he said to the woman, "Your faith has saved you; go in peace."*

—Luke 7:36-50

REFLECTING AND RECORDING

Spend a few minutes thinking about your own religious experience. Law contends
that we know so little of Jesus Christ as our Savior because we "live starving in the
coldness and deadness of a formal, historical, hearsay religion." Does that assessment
describe your experience? If not, think about what has allowed you to know Jesus as
Savior.

"We are strangers to our inward misery and wants," says Law. To what degree is that
statement true of your present situation? Prayerfully live with this thought for a few
minutes.

Recall and briefly describe an experience you have had which is most like hearing
Jesus say, "Your faith has saved you; your sins are forgiven; go in peace" (Luke 7:50,
48, 50).

If you cannot recall an experience like the one called for above, write a prayer describing to Christ how you feel right now, what your sins are, your desire for forgiveness, how you want to be delivered and be whole. Tell him that you are grateful for the salvation he offers and that you accept it.

Close your time by pondering this question: Do I "believe in a Saviour, not because [I] feel an absolute want of one, but because [I] have been told there is one, and that it would be a rebellion against God to reject him"?

DURING THE DAY

Recall the question presented above as often as possible throughout the day.

DAY
4

Never Play Leapfrog with a Unicorn

I do not want you to be unaware, brothers and sisters, that our ancestors were all under the cloud, and all passed through the sea, and all were baptized into Moses in the cloud and in the sea, and all ate the same spiritual food, and all drank the same spiritual drink. For they drank from the spiritual rock that followed them, and the rock was Christ.

Nevertheless, God was not pleased with most of them, and they were struck down in the wilderness. Now these things occurred as examples for us, so that we might not desire evil as they did. Do not become idolaters as some of them did; as it is written, "The people sat down to eat and drink, and they rose up to play." We must not indulge in sexual immorality as some of them did, and twenty-three thousand fell in a single day. We must not put Christ to the test, as some of them did, and were destroyed by serpents. And do not complain as some of them did, and were destroyed by the destroyer. These things happened to them to serve as an example, and they were written down to instruct us, on whom the ends of the ages have come. So if you think you are standing, watch out that you do not fall. No testing has overtaken you that is not common to everyone. God is faithful, and he will not let you be tested beyond your strength, but with the testing he will also provide the way out so that you may be able to endure it.

—1 Corinthians 10:1-13

You may have heard the expression "Never play leapfrog with a unicorn." We can't miss the meaning of this vivid—we might say *pointed*—image. It's a favorite teaching maxim of Alcoholics Anonymous. Recovering alcoholics and other addicts know they must separate themselves from *places* and *playmates* connected with their addiction. They must stay aware of the presence and power of temptation. The danger is greatest when the recovering person begins to feel a sense of security.

This phenomenon is relevant to all of us. The New International Version of the Bible translates verse 12 of the passage above: "So, if you think you are standing firm, be careful that you don't fall!" The exclamation mark at the end (other translations have a period) is merited. Paul wanted his words to be an exclamation, an exhortation. Overconfidence produces casualties in all walks of life—some of them spectacular. The Christian is not exempt.

The Corinthians to whom Paul was writing were convinced by their own arguments and confident in their own strength, so they were associating with pagans in their temples.

Paul knew they were headed for trouble and warned them of the danger.

But beware lest somehow this liberty of yours become a stumbling block to those who are weak. For if anyone sees you who have knowledge eating in an idol's temple, will not the conscience of him who is weak be emboldened to eat those things offered to idols?

—1 Corinthians 8:9-10

Most of the spiritual classics address this problem. Teresa of Avila writes:

The devil sets up another dangerous temptation: self-assurance in the thought that we will in no way return to our past faults and worldly pleasures: "for now I have understood the world and know that all things come to an end and that the things of God give me greater delight." If this self-assurance is present in beginners, it is very dangerous because with it a person doesn't take care against entering once more into the occasions of sin, and he falls flat: please God the relapse will not bring about something much worse. For since the devil sees that he is

dealing with a soul that can do him harm and bring profit to others, he uses all his power so that it might not rise. . . . Thus, Eternal Father, what can we do but have recourse to You and pray that these enemies of ours not lead us into temptation. . . . Prayer is a safe road; you will be more quickly freed from temptation when close to the Lord than when far. (*Soul's Passion for God*, 49–51)

Luke's account of Jesus' temptation observes that "when the devil had ended every temptation, he departed from Him until an opportune time" (Luke 4:13, NKJV). The King James Version translated that sentence: "He [the devil] departed from Him for a season." J. B. Phillips says: "The devil . . . withdrew until his next opportunity." And the New English Bible reads: "The devil departed, biding his time." This passage from Luke paints a challenging picture. The specific testing of Jesus was over. Satan knew he had lost the battle. But please note: The devil had not given up. He withdrew only to await his next opportunity. Woven through the Gospels is a continuous thread of attacks by Satan. Here is an example from Mark:

Then he began to teach them that the Son of Man must undergo great suffering, and be rejected by the elders, the chief priests, and the scribes, and be killed, and after three days rise again. He said all this quite openly. And Peter took him aside and began to rebuke him. But turning and looking at his disciples, he rebuked Peter and said, "Get behind me, Satan! For you are setting your mind not on divine things but on human things."

—Mark 8:31-33

In this case, Jesus knew the tempter was using Peter to dissuade him from taking the way of the cross and providing our salvation. If we fail to recognize this continuous battle with Satan, we will not learn lessons from Jesus that will enable us to withstand the wiles of the evil one. Mark it down: *We are never delivered from the threat of temptation.* The nature of temptation changes, but the tempter is always looking for that more opportune time.

We can never relax in overconfidence. When we think we are standing firm, "be careful that you don't fall." Teresa warns her sisters in the religious order that temptation is especially powerful when we feel safe. I would add to that the temptation is especially powerful when we are successful in our professions, even our religious professions.

I had a sad experience in the summer of 1993. I was speaking at a ministers' conference and inquired of a friend about John (not his real name), a young minister whose career I had been following for the last eight or ten years. I learned that John had just taken a leave of absence from the church. He had been appointed two years previously to a congregation once regarded as one of the leading churches in the state and served by some of the outstanding clergy of that area. Though still a strong church, it had fallen on tough times because of inadequate leadership, changing neighborhoods, and an array of problems that beset many inner-city churches. But in two years, under John's leadership, the church had been completely transformed. John is a powerful preacher, a charismatic leader in the truest sense of that word, and a caring, loving person whose ministry attracts people who are hurting and who are looking for direction. The church had become a dynamic, growing fellowship. The worship attendance had more than doubled in two years.

Then it happened: The bishop and the district superintendents received letters from a couple of women in the parish where this young man had served prior to his current appointment. The women shared painful stories of sexual indiscretions with their pastor. And so the young man was forced to withdraw from ministry, at least for a time, until he could get his life together.

Now to be sure, we don't know the whole story and we may never know it. What we do know is that this young man was successful. Everything was going his way. His ministry was being affirmed and his gifts were being used. The lesson in his story is this: Temptation and defeat often come to us when everything is going well. Sometimes even when we are at the pinnacle. You see, when we begin to think we can rely on our own power, we drop our guard. We grow lax in discipline. We no longer acknowledge our dependence upon the Lord. At the pinnacle of success, when everything is going our way, the "noonday devil" is likely to strike.

REFLECTING AND RECORDING

Can you think of an occasion in your life when you felt spiritually secure but then gave in to a temptation that filled you with guilt and shame? Record that experience here.

Teresa wrote, "Prayer is a safe road; you will be more quickly freed from temptation when close to the Lord than when far." Can you recall an experience when you were near the edge—and would have gone over the edge—of temptation if the Lord had not saved you? Record that experience here.

Look at the two experiences you have recorded. Consider your life at the time of each experience. Think about your relationship to the Lord at those times. Were you serving the Lord? Were you practicing spiritual disciplines? Ponder those experiences. What learnings can you bring out of those for the future?

DURING THE DAY

Continue to use the stanza from Charles Wesley's hymn "I Want a Principle Within" as a prayer throughout the day.

DAY
5

The Sin of Unbelief

See what love the Father has given us, that we should be called children of God; and that is what we are. The reason the world does not know us is that it did not know him. Beloved, we are God's children now; what we will be has not yet been revealed. What we do know is this: when he is revealed, we will be like him, for we will see him as he is. And all who have this hope in him purify themselves, just as he is pure.

—1 John 3:1-3

By this we know that we abide in him and he in us, because he has given us of his Spirit. And we have seen and do testify that the Father has sent his Son as the Savior of the world. God abides in those who confess that Jesus is the Son of God, and they abide in God. So we have known and believe the love that God has for us.

—1 John 4:13-16

Refusing to accept the fact that God loves you is a sin of unbelief. Julian of Norwich described this common failure powerfully:

Some of us believe that God is almighty and may do all, that God is all-wise and can do all. But that God is all love and will do all, there we fail. It is this ignorance that most hinders those who love God, as I see

it. When we begin to hate sin and amend ourselves by the ordinances of Holy Church, there remains a fear that holds us back from looking at ourselves and the sins of the past or even our everyday sins. . . . Looking at this makes us so sorry and heavy that we can scarcely see any comfort.

Sometimes we take this fear as meekness, but it is a foul blindness and weakness. We cannot despise it as we do another sin that we recognize as coming from lack of true judgment and being against truth. For of all the properties of the blessed Trinity, it is God's will that we have the most faithfulness and delight in love.

For love makes might and wisdom most meek to us. Just as God is courteous to forgive us our sin after we repent, so God wants us to forget our sin in regard to our unskillful heaviness and our doubtful fear. (*Encounter with God's Love*, 59–60)

Were Julian living today, she would address the whole issue of self-esteem, self-love, and self-appreciation or the lack thereof. One of our biggest problems is our inability to believe that God loves us.

Experiences in your past may make it difficult for you to believe that God could love you. A basic goal in counseling and therapy is to identify those barriers, those blocks to accepting love, which are based on past events. Think about your history. What experience prevents you from believing you are loved extravagantly by God? Did you have an unloving parent whom you could never please? Did the person you love the most betray you? Were you sexually abused or abused in other ways that made you feel useless? Spend some time with these questions before continuing.

❖ ❖ ❖

This sort of self-examination is helpful, but I have come to a new understanding of this dynamic. If you are wrestling with whether God loves you or not, it is a matter of confronting a sin—*the sin of unbelief*. I am not disregarding or diminishing painful experiences of your past, those relationships that reduced you to a "Norman Nothing" or a "Sally Shadow," an object rather than a person. I am simply saying that you must deal with the sin of unbelief as the starting point in addressing a lack of self-esteem. This sin is the root of your inability to accept the fact that God loves you.

I contend that refusing to accept the fact that God loves you is a sin of unbelief because the total witness of scripture is focused at this point—that God loves us with an unconditional, limitless love. Julian put it this way: "For of all the properties of the blessed Trinity, it is God's will that we have the most faithfulness and delight in love." Not only is this love the witness of scripture, but everything that Jesus said and did, climaxing with his death on the cross, is proof of God's love. The cross is the supreme revelation of love, boundless love going to the limits of crucifixion. The marvel of this love is overwhelming—that the Sinless One gladly would endure the shame and agony of the cross for miserable sinners. The outstretched arms of Christ on the cross embrace you and me, embrace all the peoples of the earth to the ends of time. If you read the Bible and if you look at the cross and you still do not accept the fact that God loves you, you are a victim of the sin of unbelief. But God forgives all our sin, including our sin of unbelief. Julian states it clearly: "Just as God is courteous to forgive us our sin after we repent, so God wants us to forget our sin in regard to our unskillful heaviness and our doubtful fear."

REFLECTING AND RECORDING

Spend a few minutes reflecting on this claim: Refusing to accept the fact that God loves you is a sin of unbelief. What relevance does this claim have for your life right now?

✦ ✦ ✦

Examine your Christian experience. Make some notes about your struggle in believing that God really loves you.

Read again the last paragraph in the passage by Julian above.

✦ ✦ ✦

If you need to forgive your own sin and give up senseless worrying and faithless fear, do so now.

✦ ✦ ✦

DURING THE DAY

Keep this thought constantly in mind throughout the day: I accept the fact that God loves me.

DAY
6

Made Fearful by Our Enemy

My brothers and sisters, whenever you face trials of any kind, consider it nothing but joy, because you know that the testing of your faith produces endurance; and let endurance have its full effect, so that you may be mature and complete, lacking in nothing. If any of you is lacking in wisdom, ask God, who gives to all generously and ungrudgingly, and it will be given you. But ask in faith, never doubting, for the one who doubts is like a wave of the sea, driven and tossed by the wind; for the doubter, being double-minded and unstable in every way, must not expect to receive anything from the Lord.

—James 1:2-8

The Greek word translated "double-minded" in this text is *dipsuchos*. The word literally means a person with two souls or two minds. One mind believes; the other disbelieves. In the double-minded person, trust and distrust of God wage a continual battle. Julian explores this struggle:

> I have understood two opposites—one is the wisest thing that anyone may do in this life, the other is the most foolish. The wisest thing is for a person to act according to the will and counsel of his greatest friend. This blessed friend is Jesus. It is his will and counsel that we should stay with him, and hold ourselves closely to him for ever, in whatever state we may be; for whether we are clean or foul it is all one to his love.

> And then we are made fearful by our enemy and through our own folly and blindness, which say to us, "You know well that you are a wretch, a sinner and faithless. You do not keep the commandments. You are always promising our Lord you will do better, and, starting right away, you fall into the same sin—especially sloth and wasting time." For this is the beginning of sin in my sight, particularly for those who have given themselves to serve God by holding [God's] blessed goodness in their hearts. (*Daily Readings*, 1:62)

Yesterday we focused on our unwillingness to believe that God loves us as the sin of unbelief. This sin is the reason for our double-mindedness. Julian explains that the contradictions within us cause us to fall into sin. Satan works on our uncertainty, our self-doubt, and our distrust of God's love. As the *father of lies* he convinces us that we are helpless sinners who can never be what God calls us to be.

Our heart-ears hear these taunts of Satan's. We pay attention because we know we have not been faithful, we have not kept the commandments, we have been timid in our witness, we have given too much attention to lust, pride has controlled our attitudes toward others, we have callously disregarded persons in need. Satan convinces us: we are "a wretch, a sinner and faithless."

Julian prescribes the only answer to double-mindedness and being made fearful by the enemy: "The wisest thing is for a person to act according to the will and counsel of his greatest friend. This blessed friend is Jesus. It is his will and counsel that we should stay with him, and hold ourselves closely to him for ever, in whatever state we may be; for whether we are clean or foul it is all one to his love."

A friend of mine Austin spent some time in prison but is now involved in a program of restitution and reconciliation. In this preventive ministry, first-time offenders are steered away from a life of crime. I met Austin while he was still in prison and was privileged to share in his coming to Christ. A portion of a letter he wrote to me speaks of the possibility open to all of us:

> Five years ago, I was released from prison after serving two and one-half years behind bars and razorwire. It is impossible to tell someone how difficult it was in prison, death threats, the hole, con air as they portray it in the movies and so many stereotypes. . . . It may be impossible for most to comprehend what one feels in captivity. I think a lot about it. I have many experiences in the military as I was a paratrooper and experienced my life in jeopardy many times. I lived my life on the edge along with my drug addiction and alcoholism.
>
> When you took me in at Christ Methodist Church as a person and not a felon I couldn't believe that one person could take in a lost soul and help mold me into one who as a Christian could also evangelize in a unique manner. . . .
>
> Most others gave up on me as an old felon with no abilities and many detriments. You didn't. . . . When you baptized me, you told the congregation that I have a story to tell. You are right, Maxie, and you are an important part of it.

Austin knows the tension and danger of double-mindedness. He has to keep reminding himself that he is a *person* for whom Christ died, not a *felon* condemned to a life of shame and regret but one who is loved and forgiven and has a ministry to fulfill.

REFLECTING AND RECORDING

Our double-mindedness is reflected in many ways. Spend two or three minutes reflecting on the degree of your double-mindedness in relation to the following pairs of opposing beliefs:

Trusting/distrusting God's love of me

✦ ✦ ✦

Trusting/distrusting God's acceptance of me

✦ ✦ ✦

Believing/doubting that I am forgiven

✦ ✦ ✦

"I'm a sinner, hopelessly lost." versus "I'm a sinner for whom Christ died, saved by his grace."

✦ ✦ ✦

"I'm not worthy to be involved in Christ's work." versus "I will serve joyfully because I am grateful for Christ's love."

✦ ✦ ✦

"Temptations are too great." versus "Greater is Christ who is within me than Satan that is in the world."

✦ ✦ ✦

DURING THE DAY

Move through the day with this constant awareness: Greater is Christ who is within me than Satan that is in the world.

D A Y

7

When We Have Fallen

"Our courteous Lord" is one of Julian's favorite titles for Jesus. In the following passage, she uses this title in describing how Christ responds to us when we sin:

> Our good Lord protects us more preciously when it seems to us that we are nearly forsaken and cast away for our sin—because we see that we have deserved it. . . .
>
> For our courteous Lord does not want his servants to despair over falling often or falling deeply. . . .This is the sovereign friendship of our courteous Lord, who protects us so tenderly while we are in our sin. Furthermore, he touches us most secretly and shows us our sin by the sweet light of mercy and grace. . . .
>
> Our courteous Lord shows himself to the soul simply and full of glad cheer, as if the soul had been in pain and in prison, saying, "My dear darling, I am glad you have come to me in all your sorrow. I have always been with you." (*Encounter with God's Love*, 37–38)

For most of us, the words *courteous* or *courtesy* do not have the meaning they once had. In a society that thinks little of civility, much less good manners, courtesy is valued little. But when we reflect a bit on its meaning, we can begin to understand Julian's preference for it.

To be courteous means to be attentive, considerate, respectful, gracious, thoughtful. It is connected with the verb "court"—to pay attention to, to allure, to charm, to seek to attract, to woo, to attempt to win the love of. No wonder Julian would talk so much about "our courteous Lord." The psalmist had a similar mind:

> *The Lord is gracious and merciful,*
> *   slow to anger and abounding in steadfast love.*
> *The Lord is good to all,*
> *   and his compassion is over all that he has made. . . .*

The Lord upholds all who are falling,
    and raises up all who are bowed down.
The eyes of all look to you,
    and you give them their food in due season.
You open your hand,
    satisfying the desire of every living thing.
The Lord is just in all his ways,
    and kind in all his doings.
The Lord is near to all who call on him,
    to all who call on him in truth.
He fulfills the desire of all who fear him;
    he also hears their cry, and saves them.
                    —Psalm 145:8-9, 14-19

Julian describes how our courteous Lord responds when we have fallen:

And when we are fallen by frailty or blindness, then our courteous Lord toucheth us, prompteth us and keepeth us. And then willeth he that we see our wretchedness, and meekly acknowledge it. But it is not his will that we busy ourselves greatly about our accusing, nor that we be too full of wretchedness about ourselves. Rather he willeth that we hastily turn unto him. . . . He hath haste to have us turn to him; for we are his joy and his delight, and he is the health of our life. . . .

Marvellous and stately is the place where the Lord dwelleth. And therefore he willeth that we readily turn us to his gracious touching, having more joy in his all-love than sorrow in our frequent fallings. (*Revelations of Divine Love*, 200, 203)

I have a friend with whom I shared intimately during our early years in the ministry. He was deeply committed to Christ and was a prophetic preacher and an effective pastor. Circumstances led him into a place and position where he exercised outstanding leadership in civil rights and racial justice. We were separated geographically, and our ministries took different expressions. Because of circumstance and geography, we drifted apart, remaining friends who kept in touch but losing the intimacy of our earlier relationship.

I still don't know the truth of what happened, but my friend left the ministry, became involved in business, made a lot of money, and is now retired. I'm not as intentional as I should be, but I try to stay in touch. I sense an emptiness in him, a longing for something he once had. In a recent long-distance conversation, soul began to touch soul, and there was deep sharing. I sensed some tears in his voice as we talked. In previous conversations, he was always overly expressive of what he had, what he was doing, where he was going—the "good life" that was his. Now there was sadness, a cautious expression of regret, but enough to prompt me to try to call him home again. I didn't use Julian's words, but I tried to say the same thing:

> **Marvellous and stately is the place where the Lord dwelleth. And therefore he willeth that we readily turn us to his gracious touching, having more joy in his all-love than sorrow in our frequent fallings.** (*Revelations of Divine Love*, 203)

He thanked me and I could feel his genuineness. I'm praying that my friend responds to our courteous Lord's invitation and returns home.

REFLECTING AND RECORDING

Spend a few minutes simply reflecting on what it means to address Christ as "our courteous Lord" and write a prayer expressing your feelings.

Julian reminds us that it is not the will of Christ that we "busy ourselves greatly about our accusing." Look at the past three or four weeks of your life—look honestly. Are you guilty of the practice or self-accusation?

✤ ✤ ✤

Julian further advises, "Nor [should] we be too full of wretchedness about ourselves." Self-despising is an ongoing pattern for some of us. How is it with you?

✤ ✤ ✤

"And when we are fallen by frailty or blindness, then our courteous Lord toucheth us, prompteth us and keepeth us. And then willeth he that we see our wretchedness, and meekly acknowledge it." Write a prayer addressing "our courteous Lord," confessing sin or failure that you are stirred to acknowledge, rejoicing in the fullness of his love and forgiveness.

DURING THE DAY

Continue to use stanza two of "I Want a Principle Within" as your prayer.

Group Meeting
for Week Two

INTRODUCTION

Participation in a group such as this is a covenant relationship. You will profit most in your daily use of this workbook if you faithfully attend these weekly meetings. Do not feel guilty if you have to miss a day in the workbook or be discouraged if you are not able to give the full thirty minutes in daily discipline. Don't hesitate to share that with the group. We learn something about ourselves when we share. You may discover, for instance, that you are unconsciously afraid of dealing with the content of a particular day because what is required will reveal something about you. Be patient with yourself and always be open to what God may be seeking to teach you.

Your growth, in part, hinges upon your group participation, so share as openly and honestly as you can and listen to what persons are saying. If you are attentive, you may pick up meaning under the surface of others' words. Being a sensitive participant in this fashion is crucial. Responding immediately to the feelings you pick up is also important. The group may need to focus its entire attention upon a particular individual at times. If some need or concern is expressed, the leader may ask the group to enter into a brief period of special prayer. But participants should not depend solely upon the leader for this kind of sensitivity. Even if you aren't the leader, don't hesitate to ask the group to join you in special prayer. This praying may be silent, or a group member may lead the group in prayer.

Remember that you have a contribution to make to the group. What you consider trivial or unimportant may be just what another person needs to hear. You need not be profound but simply share your experience. Also, if you happen to say something that is not well received or is misunderstood, don't be defensive or critical of yourself or others. Don't get diverted by overly scrutinizing your words and actions. Saint Francis de Sales says that "it is self-love which makes us anxious to know whether what we have said or done is approved or not" (*Year with the Saints*, 209).

SHARING TOGETHER

Note to leader: It may not be possible in your time frame to use all the suggestions provided each week. Select what will be most beneficial to the group. Be thoroughly familiar with these suggestions in order to move through them selectively according to the direction in which the group is moving and in consideration of the time available. Plan ahead, but do not hesitate to change your plan in response to the sharing taking place and the needs that emerge.

1. Open your time together with a brief prayer of thanksgiving for the opportunity of sharing with the group and with petitions for openness in sharing and loving response to one another.
2. Ask a volunteer to read the prayer he/she wrote on Day One, expressing commitment to being in the way of the returning prodigal.
3. Invite two or three participants who are willing to share the experience when they felt most like the prodigal son, came to themselves, realized they were lost, acknowledged that their sinful self was in control and that they needed to return to the Father (Day Two, Reflecting and Recording).
4. Invite someone to read Julian's passage at the beginning of Day Seven, then spend six to eight minutes discussing her designation of Jesus as "our courteous Lord."
5. Invite two or three persons to share the experience that was most like hearing Jesus say, "Your faith has saved you; your sins are forgiven; go in peace" (Luke 7:50; 48, 50; Day Three, Reflecting and Recording).
6. Invite someone to read Julian's word on Day Five, then spend ten to fifteen minutes discussing the contention that our doubting whether God loves us or not is a matter of sin—the sin of unbelief.
7. Invite one or two group members to share an experience when they were near the edge and would have gone over the edge of temptation if the Lord had not saved them (Day Four, Reflecting and Recording).
8. Spend eight to ten minutes discussing how our double-mindedness robs us of our energy and purpose in our Christian life.

PRAYING TOGETHER

Remember that the group's effectiveness and the quality of relationships will be enhanced by a commitment to pray for one another by name each day. If you have pictures of one another, as suggested last week, put these pictures facedown on a table and let each group member select a picture. This individual will be the focus of special prayer for the week. Bring the photos back next week, shuffle them, and draw again. Continue this process throughout your pilgrimage together. Looking at a person's picture as you pray for that person will add meaning. Having the picture also will remind you to give special prayer attention to this individual during the week.

1. Invite someone who is willing to share the prayer he/she addressed to "our courteous Lord" in Reflecting and Recording on Day Seven.
2. Praying corporately each week is a special ministry. Take some time now for a period of oral prayer. Review some of the sharing that has taken place. Now allow each group member to mention any special needs he or she wishes to share with the entire group. A good pattern is to ask for a period of prayer after each need is mentioned. The entire group may pray silently, or someone may offer a brief two-or-three-sentence oral prayer.
3. Close your time by praying together the great prayer of the church, the Lord's Prayer. As you pray this prayer, remember that you are linking yourselves with all Christians of all time in universal praise, confession, thanksgiving, and intercession.

Holiness

God Can Cleanse
and Change Our Nature

DAY
1
Gathered into Goodness

Blessed be the God and Father of our Lord Jesus Christ, who has blessed us in Christ with every spiritual blessing in the heavenly places, just as he chose us in Christ before the foundation of the world to be holy and blameless before him in love. He destined us for adoption as his children through Jesus Christ, according to the good pleasure of his will, to the praise of his glorious grace that he freely bestowed on us in the Beloved.

—Ephesians 1:3-6

In his book *Roots*, Alex Haley describes a memorable experience of the slave Kunta Kinte. Kunta drove his master to a ball at a big plantation house. When he had parked the buggy and settled down to wait out the long night of his master's revelry, he could hear the music from inside the house, the music from the white folks' dance. But then he also heard other music coming from the little cabins behind the big house. This was different music, music with a different rhythm. Something stirred within him and he found himself walking rapidly down the path toward those cabins. There a man was playing African music, music that Kunta remembered hearing when he was a child, music he had almost forgotten. He even discovered that the man who played the music was from his own part of Africa, and they were able to convrse in their native language. They later talked excitedly of home and things at home.

Kunta Kinte was changed that night. After returning from the dance, he began to reminisce about his native land and wept. He wept in sadness that he had almost forgotten home; he wept in joy that he had at last remembered. The degrading experience of slavery had almost obliterated his memory of who he was. The music was the reminder that called forth his identity.

Too much sin in our lives; too much time away from daily prayer, corporate worship, and other spiritual disciplines, these dim our self-conscious identity as Christians and dull our resolve to be holy as our God is holy. In fact, we forget that holiness is not optional for God's children. God's word is, "You shall be holy, for I am holy" (Lev. 11:45). In the passage from Ephesians quoted above, Paul contends that God the Father chose us in Christ "to be holy and blameless before him in love" (Eph. 1:4).

We have no choice if we desire to be faithful to God. The command appears burdensome, even unthinkable—that we are to be like God—until we see the call as a privilege. Yes, it is unthinkable that we should be like God, but God not only desires and commands it; God, by the gift of his spirit, provides the means whereby the unthinkable—we think impossible—can be achieved. Jesus makes the goal of Godlikeness clear: "There must be no limit to your goodness, as your heavenly Father's goodness knows no bounds" (Matt. 5:48, NEB). Julian calls us to this renewed focus on God's goodness.

> And mercy is an operation which comes from the goodness of God, and it will go on operating so long as sin is permitted to harass righteous souls. And when sin is no longer permitted to harass, then the operation of mercy will cease. And then all will be brought into righteousness and stand fast there forever. By his toleration we fall, and in his blessed love, with his power and his wisdom, we are protected, and by mercy and grace we are raised to much more joy.

> And verily and truly he will manifest to us all this marvelous joy when we shall see him. And our good Lord wants us to believe this and trust, rejoice and delight, strengthen and console ourselves, as we can with his grace and with his help, until the time that we see it in reality.

> And so long as we are in this life, whenever we in our folly revert to the contemplation of those who are damned, our Lord tenderly teaches us and blessedly calls us, saying in our souls: Leave me alone, my beloved child, attend to me. I am enough for you, and rejoice in your saviour and in your salvation. (*Showings*, 237–38, 189, 240)

REFLECTING AND RECORDING

Recall and record here your most recent experience of drifting away from the Lord. What caused the drift? What awakened you? What did it take for you to return?

Read again the last paragraph of the quotation from Julian and spend your closing time letting the truth seep into your soul.

Dᴜʀɪɴɢ ᴛʜᴇ Dᴀʏ

"Attend to me. I am enough for you, and rejoice in your saviour and in your salvation." This word of Julian is printed on page 203. Cut it out and carry it with you, reading it as often as possible.

Dᴀʏ
2

Salvation in This Life

Do not all Christians desire to have Christ to be their Saviour? Yes. But here is the deceit. All would have Christ to be their Saviour in the next world and to help them into heaven when they die, by His power and merits with God.

But this is not willing Christ to be thy Saviour; for His salvation, if it is had, must be had in this world. If He saves you, it must be done in this life, by changing and altering all that is within thee, by helping thee to a new heart, as He helped the blind to see, the lame to walk and the dumb to speak.

For to have salvation from Christ is nothing else but to be made like unto Him, it is to have His humility and meekness, His mortification and self-denial, His renunciation of the spirit, wisdom, and honors of this world, His love of God, His desire of doing God's will and seeking only His honour.

To have these tempers formed and begotten to thy heart is to have salvation from Christ. But if thou willest not to have these tempers brought forth in thee, if thy faith and desire does not seek and cry to Christ for them in the same reality as the lame asked to walk and the blind to see, then thou must be said to be unwilling to have Christ to be thy Saviour. (*Pocket William Law*, 128–29)

In this instruction, William Law is echoing Paul's exhortation to the Romans:

What then are we to say? Should we continue in sin in order that grace may abound? By no means! How can we who died to sin go on living in it? Do you not know that all of us who have been baptized into Christ Jesus were baptized into his death? Therefore we have been buried with him by baptism into death, so that, just as Christ was raised from the dead by the glory of the Father, so we too might walk in newness of life.

For if we have been united with him in a death like his, we will certainly be united with him in a resurrection like his. We know that our old self was crucified with him so that the body of sin might be destroyed, and we might no longer be enslaved to sin. For whoever has died is freed from sin. But if we have died with Christ, we believe that we will also live with him. We know that Christ, being raised from the dead, will never die again; death no longer has dominion over him. The death he died, he died to sin, once for all; but the life he lives, he lives to God. So you also must consider yourselves dead to sin and alive to God in Christ Jesus.

—Romans 6:1-11

Focus on verse 11: "So you also must consider yourselves dead to sin and alive to God in Christ Jesus." Donald Grey Barnhouse uses a rule from the sport of wrestling to help us understand this passage. To win, one wrestler must pin down the opponent's body so that two shoulders and one hip, or two hips and one shoulder, touch the mat simultaneously. If both hips but neither shoulder are on the mat; or if both shoulders and neither hip are on the mat, that is not enough. There is yet no mastery, no winner. Barnhouse points out that, as believers, we may admit that we have been grievously thrown, and even sorely wounded, "even as one wrestler may seize the other and throw him over his shoulder; but there is no mastery" (*Romans*, III: 130). If we stay true to our spiritual disciplines, when we sin we will immediately repent, preventing sin from any mastery in our life.

Paul wrote to the Thessalonians, "It is God's will that you should be sanctified" (1 Thess. 4:3, NIV). To be sanctified is to be made holy. From the time we believe in Jesus, repent and accept him as Savior, we are set apart for God, set apart to be *holy*. By a miracle of God's grace, no matter the depths of sin we may have experienced, we can be made holy. Living and behaving like people set apart by God is not easy. That is the reason we must remember that in *position*, in relationship to sin and to Christ, we are dead to sin and alive to Christ. We will consider this idea further tomorrow.

REFLECTING AND RECORDING

When you are quiet and still, the Lord can speak to your hearts. Be quiet and still now. Imagine that you are alone. Christ comes to you, looks at you in love, and says, "Why have you forsaken me, when I have never abandoned you?" Why would Jesus say that to you? Make some notes, indicating your recent actions and attitudes that would cause Jesus to think you may have forsaken him.

Now listen again to Christ. Imagine him saying, "I will never leave you either in joy or sorrow, in sin or in failure. I will always be here to help and watch over you. Nothing can separate you from me." Write a brief prayer of thanksgiving in response to Christ.

DURING THE DAY

Continue to read and reflect as often as possible on the word from Julian you clipped yesterday.

DAY
3

The Process of Sanctification

Read Romans 6:1-11, on which we concentrated yesterday.

❖ ❖ ❖

Now consider Romans 6:12-14 in J. B. Phillips's translation, *The New Testament in Modern English*.

Do not, then, allow sin to establish any power over your mortal bodies in making you give way to your lusts. Nor hand over your bodily parts to be, as it were, weapons of evil for the devil's purposes. But, like [ones] rescued from certain death, put yourselves in God's hands as weapons of good for [God's] own purposes. For sin can never be your master—you are no longer living under the Law, but under grace.

Two dimensions of our salvation are justification and sanctification. The classic orthodox doctrine of Protestant Christianity is that we are justified by grace through faith. Paul expressed this concept in Romans 3:23-25 (NKJV):

For all have sinned and fall short of the glory of God, being justified freely by His grace through the redemption that is in Christ Jesus, whom God set forth to be a propitiation by His blood, through faith, to demonstrate His righteousness, because in His forbearance God had passed over the sins that were previously committed.

Thinking of *justification* as a legal metaphor, we would say that in God's court, we are utterly guilty. Yet, in amazing mercy, God *treats* us, *reckons* us, *accounts* us, as innocent. In our relationship with God, we are accepted as though we were without sin.

Sanctification is the process by which we are perfected in love. In Paul's words, it is growing up into Christian maturity, "to the measure of the full stature of Christ" (Eph. 4:13) or yielding ourselves so completely "until Christ is formed in you" (Gal. 4:19).

The ongoing dynamic of the Christian life is to work out *in fact* what is already true *in principle*. *In position*, in our relation to God in Jesus Christ, we are new persons—that is justification. Now our *condition*, the actual life we live, must be brought into harmony with our new position—that is the process of sanctification. Writers of the spiritual classics across the centuries passionately call us to sanctification. Here is a plea from Julian of Norwich:

> The highest bliss there is, is to possess God in the clarity of endless light, truly seeing him, sweetly feeling him, peacefully possessing him in the fulness of joy; and a part of this blessed aspect of our Lord God was revealed. In this revelation I saw that sin was the greatest opposition to this, so much so that as long as we have anything to do with any kind of sin, we shall never clearly see the blessed face of God. . . .
>
> [H]e will never have his full joy in us until we have our full joy in him, truly seeing his fair, blessed face.
>
> And so I hope that by his grace he lifts up and will draw our outer disposition to the inward, and will make us all at unity with him, and each of us with others in the true, lasting joy which is Jesus. (*Showings*, 320, 318–19)

A serious young man once sought counsel from a rabbi. The rabbi asked him, "What have you done all your life?" The seeker replied, "I have gone through the whole of the Talmud three times." The rabbi studied his visitor, then inquired: "Yes, but how much of the Talmud has gone through you?" (Read, 3 April, 1999, in *Words of Life*).

Sanctification requires that we allow Christ to possess us completely in the fullness of joy, ferreting out our fears, freeing us from self-protection and self-centeredness, illuminating and delivering us from sin. "For sin can never be your master—you are no longer living under the Law, but under grace" (Rom. 6:14, JBPHILLIPS)

REFLECTING AND RECORDING

Spend a few minutes reflecting on the following translations of Romans 6:14:

"Sin will have no dominion over you." (NRSV)

⊹ ⊹ ⊹

"Sin shall not be lord over you." (Weymouth)

⊹ ⊹ ⊹

"You must not give sin a vote in the way you conduct your lives." (THE MESSAGE)

"Do not, then, allow sin to establish any power over your mortal bodies in making you give way to your lusts." (JBPHILLIPS)

Go back and read the paragraph on *justification*. Do you consider yourself justified?

Go back and read the paragraph on *sanctification*. Spend the balance of your time in this session pondering where you are on the road or in your commitment to sanctification.

DURING THE DAY

Continue reflecting on the word from Julian of Norwich, which you cut out on Day One.

DAY
4

The Burden of a Great Potential

Charles Schulz, the cartoonist who gave us *Peanuts*, is one of my favorite theologians. That may say something about the kind of theological seminary president I am. His cartoons relate to the human condition, many of them speaking a biblical message.

In one series, Linus, in a pensive mood, speaks to Charlie Brown: "Everyone's so upset because I didn't make the honor roll." He becomes agitated as he continues,

"My mother's upset, my father's upset, my teacher's upset, the principal's upset. Good grief!" He then explains to Charlie Brown, "They all say the same thing . . . they're disappointed because I have such potential." In the final frame, he screams, "There's no heavier burden than a great potential!"

Potential may be a burden, but it also is a blessing, particularly in terms of spiritual development. According to Brother Lawrence :

All things are possible to [one] who believes;
they are less difficult to [one]who hopes.
they are more easy to [one]who loves, and still more easy to [one]who perseveres in the practice of these three virtues.

The end we ought to propose to ourselves is to become, in this life, the most perfect worshipers of God we can possibly be, as we hope to be through all eternity.

The greater perfection a soul aspires after, the more dependent it is upon divine grace. (*Practice of the Presence*, 21–22)

Brother Lawrence sounds themes common among writers of our spiritual classics:

- practicing holy habits
- aspiring for perfection
- cultivating virtues
- persevering in discipline
- seeking holiness

Many write in the spirit of the writer of Hebrews:

Endure trials for the sake of discipline. God is treating you as children; for what child is there whom a parent does not discipline? If you do not have that discipline in which all children share, then you are illegitimate and not his children. Moreover, we had human parents to discipline us, and we respected them. Should we not be even more willing to be subject to the Father of spirits and live? For they disciplined us for a short time as seemed best to them, but he disciplines us for our good, in order that we may share his holiness. Now, discipline always seems painful rather than pleasant at the time, but later it yields the peaceful fruit of righteousness to those who have been trained by it.
—Hebrews 12:7-11

In our reading from Julian yesterday, she says, "I saw that sin was the greatest opposition to this, so much so that as long as we have anything to do with any kind of sin, we shall never clearly see the blessed face of God." Underscore the fact: Holiness is not optional for Christians. We are called to holiness. There should be about us Christians something distinctive

- in the way we do our work;
- in the way we relate to our spouses;

- in the way we rear our children;
- in the way we relate to our parents;
- in the way we care for the poor;
- in the way we witness and share the gospel;
- in our personal morality;
- in our ethical commitments;
- in the way we spend our money.

Our aim is holiness. We translate the Greek word *hagiasmos* as "holy." The root meaning of the Greek word is always *difference* and *separation*. We are to be "in the world but not of the world." The standards of the world are not our standards. Our aim is to please God, not other people. Paul called the Philippians, and us, to "be blameless and innocent, children of God without blemish in the midst of a crooked and perverse generation, in which you shine like stars in the world" (2:15).

The New Testament scholar B. F. Westcott says that holiness is "the preparation for the presence of God" (quoted in Barclay, *Daily Study Bible*, 207). Brother Lawrence would agree. "The greater perfection a soul aspires after, the more dependent it is upon divine grace."

REFLECTING AND RECORDING

Read again the suggested areas in which Christians must be distinctive. Concentrate on each one, asking yourself if there is something distinctive in that dimension of your life.

DURING THE DAY

Keep careful note of the way you move through the day—doing your work, relating to others, witnessing. What is your attitude to persons of other ethnic and economic groups? How do you make your moral decisions? Is there anything distinctively "holy" about the way you live?

DAY
5

Dependent upon Divine Grace

Read again Hebrews 12:7-11, which we considered yesterday, then the continuation here.

Therefore lift your drooping hands and strengthen your weak knees, and make straight paths for your feet, so that what is lame may not be put out of joint, but rather be healed. Pursue peace with everyone, and the holiness without which no one will see the Lord. See to it that no one fails to obtain the grace of God; that no root of bitterness springs up and causes trouble, and through it many become defiled. See to it that no one becomes like Esau, an immoral and godless person, who sold his birthright for a single meal. You know that later, when he wanted to inherit the blessing, he was rejected, for he found no chance to repent, even though he sought the blessing with tears.

—Hebrews 12:12-17

Yesterday's reading from Brother Lawrence concluded, "The greater perfection a soul aspires after, the more dependent it is upon divine grace." Without God's grace, holiness is impossible. Charles H. Spurgeon put it bluntly, "A man might as well hope to hold the north wind in the hollow of his hand as expect to control by his own strength those boisterous powers which dwell within his fallen nature" (*All of Grace*, 33). Spurgeon goes on to say:

Salvation would be a sadly incomplete affair if it did not deal with this part of our ruined estate. We want to be purified as well as pardoned. Justification without sanctification would not be salvation at all. It would call the leper clean, and leave him to die of his disease; it would forgive the rebellion and allow the rebel to remain an enemy to his king. It would remove the consequences but overlook the cause, and this would leave an endless and hopeless task before us. (*All of Grace*, 34)

Brother Lawrence addresses our journey toward holiness in this way:

Our good sister ——— . . . seems to me full of good will, but she wants to go faster than grace. One does not become holy all at once. I commend her to you. . . .

I am filled with shame and confusion when I reflect, on one hand, upon the great favors which God has bestowed and is still bestowing upon me; and, on the other, upon the ill use I have made of them, and my small advancement in the way of perfection. . . .

We cannot escape the dangers which abound in life without the actual and continual help of God. Let us, then, pray to Him for it continually. How can we pray to Him without being with Him? How can we be with Him but in thinking of Him often? And how can we often think of Him unless by a holy habit of thought which we should form? (*Conversations and Letters*, 38–39)

The holy habit we must form in order to know holiness is constant dependence upon God's grace. We can't change our own heart or cleanse our own nature. But God can. Here is God's promise: "I will make them and the region around my hill a blessing; and I will send down the showers in their season; they shall be showers of blessing" (Ezek. 34:26).

The passage from Hebrews above notes the danger of *missing the grace of God* or *failing to obtain* God's grace. We must be vigilant. By our thoughtlessness, through our lethargy, or because of our procrastination, we may not keep ourselves in the stream of God's grace. But that is our fault and our responsibility. God is faithful. While we cannot, in our own power, transform our fallen nature and reverse the direction of our desires, God can. Spurgeon says it so well:

Did it ever strike you what a wonderful thing it is for the Lord to give a new heart and a right spirit to a [person]? You have seen a lobster, perhaps, which has fought with another lobster, and lost one of its claws, and a new claw has grown. That is a remarkable thing; but it is a much more astounding fact that a [person] should have a new heart given to him [or her]. This, indeed, is a miracle beyond the powers of nature. There is a tree. If you cut off one of its limbs, another one may grow in its place; but can you change its nature; can you sweeten sour sap; can you make the thorn bear figs? You can graft something better into it, and that is the analogy which nature gives us of the work of grace; but absolutely to change the vital sap of the tree would be a miracle indeed. Such a prodigy and mystery of power God works in all who believe in Jesus.

If you yield yourself up to His divine working, the Lord will alter your nature; He will subdue the old nature, and breathe new life into you. (*All of Grace*, 38–39)

During the early sixties I had a shocking realization: *I am as holy as I want to be.* I was a young Methodist preacher in Mississippi, organizing pastor of a congregation that had known amazing growth and success. My involvement in the civil rights movement then splintered the fellowship of that congregation. There was nothing radical about my involvement, but many folks in the church could not understand my commitment and participation. I couldn't understand their lack of understanding. The gospel seemed clear.

The pressure, stress, and tension wore me out. I was physically, emotionally, and spiritually exhausted when I went to a retreat (a Christian ashram) led by the world-famous missionary-evangelist E. Stanley Jones. I will never forget going to the altar to have Brother Stanley "lay on hands" and pray for my healing. He knew my story, and as I knelt, he asked, "Do you want to be whole?" That was one of those sanctifying experiences of my life, changing the direction of my ministry. My challenge was to allow Christ to minister *through* me rather than struggling to minister *for* Christ.

Through the years I have changed the final word in the question, though the meaning is pretty much the same. I am constantly asking myself, "Do I want to be holy?" and constantly reminding myself that I am as holy as I want to be. Years later I read in Thomas Kepler's *A Journey with the Saints* the story of two students from Paris who once visited Jan van Ruysbroeck to learn spiritual truth. After their conversation, the two left dissatisfied, for Ruysbroeck had said to them, "You will be as holy as you wish to be" (Kepler, *Journey with the Saints*, 29).

To the degree that we are willing to yield ourselves to the transforming working of the indwelling Christ, he will alter our nature, subdue our old nature, and continue giving us new life.

REFLECTING AND RECORDING

On Day Three of this week, we considered the two dimensions of salvation: justification and sanctification. Sanctification requires that we allow Christ to possess us completely. We have *desire* and *will* that he possess us. That's what I experienced with E. Stanley Jones. Can you recall a similar experience? Record that experience here.

Write a prayer of commitment, expressing your willingness to allow Christ to possess you completely.

DURING THE DAY

Repeat Day Four's instructions for During the Day.

DAY
6

Pride and Humility:
One Is Death; the Other, Life

The heart knows its own bitterness,
and no stranger shares its joy.
The house of the wicked is destroyed,
but the tent of the upright flourishes.
There is a way that seems right to a person,
but its end is the way to death.
Even in laughter the heart is sad,
and the end of joy is grief.
The perverse get what their ways deserve,
and the good, what their deeds deserve.
—Proverbs 14:10-14

Holiness is not optional for God's people. At the heart of holiness is humility—the virtue of knowing who we are, especially in relation to God. When we keep company with the saints, they teach us that pride is destructive and humility is saving. William Law goes so far as to say pride means death; humility means life.

Give up yourselves to the meek and humble spirit of the holy Jesus, the overcomer of all fire and pride and wrath. This is the one way, the one truth and the one life. There is no other open door into the sheepfold of God. Everything else is the working of the devil in the fallen nature of [humanity].

Humility must sow the seed, or there can be no reaping in heaven. Look not at pride only as an unbecoming temper; nor at humility only as a decent virtue; for the one is death and the other is life; the one is hell and the other is all heaven.

So much as you have of pride, so much you have of the fallen angel alive in you; so much as you have of true humility, so much you have of the Lamb of God within you. "Learn of me for I am meek and lowly of heart." If this lesson is unlearnt, we must be said to have left our Master, as those disciples did who went back and walked no more with him. (*Joy of the Saints*, 235)

When we consider pride, we are not talking about something simply unbecoming to our temper and character. When we talk about humility, we are not affirming a decent virtue. These are issues of life and death, heaven and hell. William Law echoes the proverb: "There is a way that seems right to a person, but its end is the way of death" (14:12).

I have a friend who has learned this lesson through great pain. She has discovered the destructive results of going her own way in pride, setting herself up as the arbiter and judge of right and wrong, seeking only that which she thinks would bring happiness. I had been her pastor and I knew some of her story—more than she thought I knew. I had moved and had not seen her since she left her husband and two sons six months previously. I returned to preach in her city, which inspired her to write a letter of honest confession and sharing:

So much has happened to me. I would like to tell you about it. You know, of course, about my affair and my choosing to leave [my husband]. What you may not know is that the man I loved and trusted and essentially gave up everything and everyone for, just played with me, relieved me of about $30,000, found someone he liked much better, and with absolutely no warning—left. Poof! My head is still spinning. I have managed to "get up," but I am still in the process of "dusting myself off."

You may have little experience with big sins, so I will tell you an interesting thing that I have noticed. A sinner can justify anything. I managed, as I was thoroughly enjoying my affair, to believe that God sent this man to me . . . that He put us together so that each of us could be happy at last, after long years of unhealthy and unhappy marriages. And furthermore, that each of us would be better people because we now had reason to rejoice.

There is no justification for dishonest, hurtful behavior. And I am facing the consequences of my behavior. I am not sad that I am no longer married to _____, but I am so very sorry to have left that marriage in such a destructive way. And how I hurt my children and my mother and siblings! What a mess. Still, I wonder if I had ever had a lucid moment, if I had ever asked myself if this was really something I was willing to put my children through, if I had asked myself if I was willing to live with such disappointing behavior . . . would I have rallied and put an end to the affair? I don't think so. I was like the Titanic headed for the iceberg. . . full steam ahead. I listened to no one, I accepted no advice, I thought I knew this man better than anyone and only I understood how fine he was.

I am humbled. I am humbled in two ways. I am humbled at how wrong I could be. I am concerned about my judgment, in general.

REFLECTING AND RECORDING

Recall and record an experience when you went your own way in pride, set yourself up as the arbiter and judge of right and wrong, sought only that which you thought would bring happiness—but it brought unhappiness, even destruction. It doesn't have to be as dramatic as my friend's folly. If you can't recall a personal experience, make some notes about an experience of someone you know.

Spend the balance of your time reflecting on Law's assertion that pride is death, humility is life; pride is hell, humility is heaven.

DURING THE DAY

Memorize and take this proverb with you in the days ahead:

> *There is a way that seems right to a person,*
> *But its end is the way of death.*
>   —Proverbs 14:12

DAY
7

The Peril of Overconfidence

For I do not want you to be ignorant of the fact . . . that our [forebears] were all under the cloud and that they all passed through the sea. They were all baptized into Moses in the cloud and in the sea. They all ate the same spiritual food and drank the same spiritual drink; for they drank from the spiritual rock that accompanied them, and that rock was Christ. Nevertheless, God was not pleased with most of them; their bodies were scattered over the desert.

Now these things occurred as examples to keep us from setting our hearts on evil things as they did. Do not be idolaters, as some of them were; as it is written: "The people sat down to eat and drink and got up to indulge in pagan revelry." We should not commit sexual immorality, as some of them did—and in one day twenty-three thousand of them died. We should not test the Lord, as some of them did—and were killed by snakes. And do not grumble, as some of them did—and were killed by the destroying angel.

These things happened to them as examples and were written down as warnings for us, on whom the fulfillment of the ages has come. So, if you think you are standing firm, be careful that you don't fall! No temptation has seized you except what is common to man. And God is faithful; he will not let you be tempted beyond what you can bear. But when you are tempted, he will also provide a way out so that you can stand up under it.

—1 Corinthians 10:1-13, NIV

Seldom do you find an exclamation point in the Bible. Check it out in the translation you use. Note the New International Version's exclamation mark closing a sentence in the last paragraph quoted above. Paul wanted this sentence to grab our attention. "So, if you think you are standing firm, be careful that you don't fall!" J. B. Phillips doesn't use an exclamation point, but his translation is a graphic expression: "So let the man who feels sure of his standing today be careful that he does not fall *tomorrow*" (emphasis mine).

Overconfidence produces its casualties in all walks of life, some quite spectacular. Christians are no exception. I have a friend who spent five years in prison. I shared a part of his story on Day Six of Week Two. He was in prison with Jim Bakker, the televangelist who hosted "PTL" ("Praise the Lord") on TV and was convicted of misusing millions of dollars, dollars given to support ministry but used instead for Bakker's personal agenda. Bakker confessed to my friend, and since his release, has talked publicly about becoming overconfident and seeing himself as a kind of "law unto himself."

You don't have to look long at Paul's life to understand why he would sound this warning: "If you think you are standing firm, be careful that you don't fall!" (1 Cor. 10:12). In the history of Christianity, few have lived more adventurously and taken more risks. On one occasion, he catalogs his trials and tribulations:

> *Are they ministers of Christ?—I speak as a fool—I am more: in labors more abundant, in stripes above measure, in prisons more frequently, in death often. From the Jews five times I received forty stripes minus one. Three times I was beaten with rods; once I was stoned; three times I was shipwrecked; a night and a day I have been in the deep; in journeys often, in perils of waters, in perils of robbers, in perils of my own countrymen, in perils of the Gentiles, in perils in the city, in perils in the wilderness, in perils in the sea, in perils among false brethren; in weariness and toil, in sleeplessness often, in hunger and thirst, in fastings often, in cold and nakedness—besides the other things, what comes upon me daily: my deep concern for all the churches. Who is weak, and I am not weak? Who is made to stumble, and I do not burn with indignation?*

> —2 Corinthians 11:23-29, NKJV

Can't you imagine how often physical weakness and emotional strain exposed Paul to the assaults of Satan? He was confident but not overconfident. He turned his weakness into a channel for appropriating strength, because he learned to trust and depend on Christ. Teresa warns against *overconfidence* by exposing our proclivity for *self-deception*:

> Let us now come to the time of trial—for we can only test ourselves by watching our actions narrowly, and we shall soon detect signs of deceptions.

> For instance as regards humility. We fancy we do not wish for honour and that we are indifferent to everything of the kind—yet let anyone offer us the slightest affront, and our feelings and behaviour will at once betray that we are not humble.

> Besides, if any opportunity occurs of augmenting our dignity we do not reject it for

the sake of a greater good. And God grant we may not seek such honour.

We are so accustomed to saying that we want nothing and are indifferent to everything (which we really believe is the fact), that at last the very habit of asserting it convinces us of its truth more strongly.

It is wise to be aware that this is a temptation for when God gives us any solid virtue it brings all the others in its train.
(*Living Water*, 48)

REFLECTING AND RECORDING

Read the passage above from Teresa carefully. Rewrite paragraphs two, three, and four in your own words in the space to the right of the texts.

❖   ❖   ❖

Can you recall an experience when you failed in an endeavor or fell into sin because of overconfidence? Make enough notes here to recall and record that experience.

Can you recall an experience of self-deception that brought failure or pain or a damaged relationship? Record that experience here.

Close your time in prayer, asking the Lord to forgive known sins in your life and to heal any broken relationships.

DURING THE DAY

The Lord's Prayer has the petition: "Save us from the time of trial, and deliver us from evil." Take that petition with you through this day.

Group Meeting
for Week Three

INTRODUCTION

Two essential ingredients for a Christian fellowship are feedback and follow-up. Feedback keeps the group dynamic working positively for all participants. Follow-up expresses Christian concern and ministry.

The leader is the one primarily responsible for feedback in the group, but all members should be encouraged to share their feelings about how the group is functioning. Listening is crucial. Listening to one another, as much as any other action, is a means of affirming the other. When we listen to another, we are saying, "You are important; I value you." Being sure we understand the meaning of what others say is critical too. We often mishear. "Are you saying _____?" is a good question to check what we heard. If a couple of persons in a group listen and give feedback in this fashion, they can set the mood for the whole group.

Follow-up is a function for everyone. If we listen to what others are saying, we will discover needs and concerns beneath the surface, situations that deserve special prayer and attention. Make notes of these as the group shares. Follow up during the week with a telephone call, a written note of caring and encouragement, maybe a visit. What distinguishes Christian fellowship is caring in action. "My, how those Christians love one another!"

Saint Augustine said, "All our good and all our evil certainly lies in the character of our actions. As they are, so are we; for we are the tree, and they the fruit, and therefore, they prove what each one is" (*Year with the Saints*, 227). So follow up each week with others in the group.

By this time you are getting to know one another pretty well; a significant amount of "knowing" exists in the group. Persons are beginning to feel safe in the group and perhaps more willing to share. Still there is no place for pressure. The leader, however, can be especially sensitive to those slow to share. Seek to coax them out gently. Every individual is a gift to the group. The gift is fully revealed by sharing.

1. Begin your time together by singing a chorus or stanza from a hymn everyone knows, such as "Amazing Grace."

2. Spend eight to ten minutes letting each participant talk about "how I'm doing" with this workbook. What is positive? negative? Are there special meanings? joys? difficulties? Encourage one another.

3. Invite someone to read the passage from William Law on Day Two. Spend eight to twelve minutes discussing Law's claim that Christ's salvation "if it is had, must be had in this world."

4. On Day Four we considered the call to holiness and the call that we be distinctive as Christians. Turn to that day in your workbook and look at each of the areas in which Christian signs should identify us. Spend ten to fifteen minutes talking about your successes and failures in these areas.

5. Invite two or three persons to share an experience similar to the one the author described on Day Five—a sanctifying experience. When did these individuals desire and express willingness for Christ to possess them completely?

6. In light of this sharing (question 5), spend ten to twelve minutes discussing and clarifying the meaning of justification and sanctification. Speak personally and honestly.

7. On Day Six we explored the complementary themes that pride brings death and humility brings life. You read a dramatic testimony of pride's bringing "death" for the woman who left her family and were asked to recall and record an expression of personal unhappiness, even destruction. Would one or two participants be willing to share that experience?

8. Invite someone to read his or her "translation" of the passage by Teresa on Day Seven.

9. Invite one or two persons to share an experience when overconfidence caused them to fail in an endeavor.

10. Invite one or two group members to share an experience of self-deception that brought failure, pain, or a damaged relationship.

PRAYING TOGETHER

1. The leader takes up the photos of the group members, shuffles them, and lets each person draw a new one.

2. Invite each member of the group to spend two minutes in quiet prayer for the person whose picture he or she has drawn, focusing on what the individual has shared in this meeting.

3. Invite group members to look at the prayers of thanksgiving they wrote on Day Two; then ask as many as will to offer brief prayers on behalf of persons who have shared special needs in this session. The leader will offer a final prayer.

A WORD OF ENCOURAGEMENT

William Law's feelings about beginning the day with prayer are expressed in the words of Richard C. Trench:

> Lord, what a change within us one short hour
> Spent in Thy presence will avail to make!
> What heavy burdens from our bosoms take!
> What parched grounds refresh as with a shower!
> We kneel, and all around us seems to lower;
> We rise, and all, the distant and the near,
> Stands forth in sunny outline, brave and clear;
> We kneel, how weak! We rise, how full of power!
> (Kepler, *Journey with the Saints*, 81)

Prayer

The Soul Wholly
Given to God

DAY
1

Keeping Humility in Perspective

Now so it was, as the multitude pressed about Him to hear the word of God, that He stood by the Lake of Gennesaret, and saw two boats standing by the lake; but the fishermen had gone from them and were washing their nets. Then He got into one of the boats, which was Simon's, and asked him to put out a little from the land. And He sat down and taught the multitudes from the boat. Now when He had stopped speaking, He said to Simon, "Launch out into the deep and let down your nets for a catch."

But Simon answered and said to Him, "Master, we have toiled all night and caught nothing; nevertheless at Your word I will let down the net." And when they had done this, they caught a great number of fish, and their net was breaking. So they signaled to their partners in the other boat to come and help them. And they came and filled both the boats, so that they began to sink. When Simon Peter saw it, he fell down at Jesus' knees, saying, "Depart from me, for I am a sinful man, O Lord!"

—Luke 5:1-8, NKJV

Pride and humility are consistent themes with spiritual writers. They all agree: Pride is one of the greatest barriers, and humility is an absolute essential in our relationship to God. On Day Six of Week Three, we considered William Law's claim that pride means death and humility means life. He also said, "Love has no more of pride, than light has of darkness; it stands and bears all its fruits from a depth, and root of humility" (*Spirit of Prayer*, Pryr-2.3-9).

As we come into the presence of Christ, there is always some reservation, a quivering inside. Many times we cower because of deep feelings of unworthiness. When Jesus directed Peter and his companions to a source of abundant fish after their all-night effort had yielded nothing, he got Peter's attention. Jesus proved his power in the arena of nature and of the work where Peter was a master. Peter was overwhelmed by a sense of divine power and love, which made him feel small and unworthy.

I've been there—times when I felt I couldn't bear to be in Jesus' presence. I remember a prayer meeting in a hotel room in Beijing in 1978. The Bamboo Curtain was being pulled back just slightly. Most Chinese Christians still were practicing their faith and worshiping underground. In fact, it was dangerous for Christians in that country to meet with Americans. Three Christian couples braved exposure, meeting with a group of American Christians of which I was one. These couples had suffered for their faith—husbands and wives separated for long years, as they were being reeducated for the Communist kingdom. Two of them had been tortured almost to death. As we prayed, it was obvious that these persons were in a relationship with Jesus far deeper than I had ever imagined possible. Christ was present in that room in such a real way that I felt I couldn't bear it. My own limited life of faith and limited experience with Jesus were made glaringly real. I wanted to cry out with Peter, "Depart from me, for I am a sinful man, O Lord."

There have been other experiences. Recently I had a conversation with a young couple who were graduating from seminary. Their excitement was contagious. They talked of their return to Bangladesh as missionaries with their three children. I knew the setting into which they were going, the hardship and danger. But they couldn't wait. They were on the edge of their seats with excitement as they shared their understanding of God's call. Their faces were radiant. I felt I was on a kind of Mount of Transfiguration with this young couple and Jesus. Instead of wanting to build tabernacles to stay there, though, I had an urge to run away. There was something in their commitment, in their willingness to risk everything—including family—for the sake of the kingdom that made me uneasy—that challenged my own discipleship. I knew I was in the presence of Jesus and I quivered inside. Deep feelings of unworthiness began to rise within me.

Teresa of Avila insists that kind of feeling of humility is essential for prayer.

God is well pleased to see a soul humbly taking His Son as Mediator, and yet loving Him so much that, even if His Majesty is pleased to raise it to the highest contemplation, as I have said, it realizes its unworthiness, and says with Saint Peter: "Depart from me, Lord, for I am a sinful man." I have proved this, for it is in this way that God has led my soul. Others, as I have said, will take another and a shorter road. What I have learned is this: that the entire foundation of prayer must be established in humility, and that, the more a soul abases itself in prayer, the higher God raises it. I do not remember that He has ever granted me any of the outstanding favours of which I shall speak later save when I have been consumed with shame by realizing my own wickedness; and His Majesty has even managed to help me to know myself by revealing to me things which I myself could not have imagined. (*Complete Works of Saint Teresa*, I:141)

REFLECTING AND RECORDING

Recall and record here an experience when you were overwhelmed by Christ's presence, maybe fearful, and did not feel worthy to be there. Describe the experience in enough detail to remember and relive it.

With this memory as your experiential base, spend a few minutes reflecting on Teresa's claim, "What I have learned is this: that the entire foundation of prayer must be established in humility, and that, the more a soul abases itself in prayer, the higher God raises it."

❖　❖　❖

Rewrite Teresa's sentence above in your own words.

DURING THE DAY

Many Christians know the Lord's Prayer by memory. This prayer is printed on page 203. If you do not know it by memory, clip it out and carry it with you today. See how many times you can deliberately pray this prayer.

DAY
2

Prayer As Dominant Desire

Now you are the body of Christ and individually members of it. And God has appointed in the church first apostles, second prophets, third teachers; then deeds of power, then gifts of healing, forms of assistance, forms of leadership, various kinds of tongues. Are all apostles? Are all prophets? Are all teachers? Do all work miracles? Do all possess gifts of healing? Do all speak in tongues? Do all interpret? But strive for the greater gifts. And I will show you a still more excellent way. If I speak in the tongues of mortals and of angels, but do not have love, I am a noisy gong or a clanging cymbal.

—1 Corinthians 12:27–13:1

Most of us know what follows in 1 Corinthians 13—the great hymn of love. We don't know the reason for a break in the text between chapters twelve and thirteen. Because there is a break and because we tend to read the Bible in chapters, we may miss an important lesson. The thirteenth chapter on love is an explanation of verse 31 of chapter 12: "But strive for the greater gifts. And I will show you a still more excellent way."

In chapter 12, Paul has been speaking of spiritual gifts, insisting that "each is given the manifestation of the Spirit for the common good" (verse 7). He talks about the gifts of knowledge, faith, healing, prophecy, discernment, tongues. He also gives us that powerful metaphor of the church as a body, making the case that every member, however gifted, is essential for the body to function as a whole. He concludes that discussion with the verses printed above, urging us to "strive for the greater gifts." Another translation reads, "earnestly desire the greater gifts" (NASB).

One of our problems with prayer is failure to realize that *what we desire most is our deepest prayer.* William Law makes a more expansive claim: "All our natural tempers . . . are . . . in reality only so many different kinds . . . of prayer."

Every [one's] life is a continual state of prayer; he [or she] is no moment free from it, nor can possibly be so. For all our natural tempers, be they what they will, ambition, covetousness, selfishness, worldly-mindedness, pride, envy, hatred, malice, or any other lust whatever, are all of them in reality, only so many different kinds, and forms of a spirit of prayer, which is as inseparable from the heart, as weight is from the body. For every natural temper is nothing else, but a manifestation of the desire and prayer of the heart, and shows us, how it works and wills. And as the heart worketh, and willeth, such, and no other, is its prayer. . . . If therefore the working desire of the heart is not habitually turned towards God, if this is not our spirit of prayer, we are necessarily in a state of prayer towards something else, that carries us from God, and brings all kind of Evil into us. . . . Pray we must, as sure as our heart is alive; and therefore when the state of our heart is not a spirit of prayer to God, we pray without ceasing to some, or other part of the creation. (*Spirit of Prayer*, Pryr-2.3-23)

Paul urged the Thessalonians to pray without ceasing (1 Thess. 5:17). Tomorrow we will consider that call to a discipline of intention and attention. Today, consider the truth that there is a sense in which we do pray without ceasing, without thought of it. Harry Emerson Fosdick challenges us with his discussion of "prayer as dominant desire." He refers to Jesus' story of the importunate widow, the woman who kept coming to a judge day after day, demanding justice. Finally, because of her persistence, the judge responds (Luke 18:1-8). Then Fosdick adds,

Not alone the woman who pleads with the reluctant judge for justice, but the prodigal seeking from his father the means of dissipation, is praying; and any [one] who after money or fame or pleasure insistently directs his [or her] course, has in his [or her] dominant desire the prayer that shapes his [or her] life. We must accept for a while the fruitful definition which Mrs. Browning gives us, "Every *wish*, with God, is a prayer."

One immediate result of this point of view is a clear perception that *everybody is praying*. Prayer regarded as a definite act of approach to God may be shut out from any life. But prayer regarded as desire, exercised in any realm and for anything, at once includes us all. In this general sense we pray without ceasing. (*Meaning of Prayer*, 143)

One of the shocking insights intrinsic to this understanding is that while prayer may be regarded as the act of our best thoughts and desires, we are praying in our worst hours too.

Prayer may be either heavenly or devilish. . . . None ever found heaven, here or anywhere, without prayer—the uplift of a settled desire after God and righteousness. And none ever found hell, here or anywhere, without prayer—the dead set and insistent craving of the heart after evil. In any group . . . , you may not in this sense divide those who pray from those who do not. All are praying the prayer of dominant desire. The great question is: what are they after? what is their demand on life? (*Meaning of Prayer*, 137)

I make my own witness. My wife, Jerry, and I decided to purchase a condominium on the beach, which, in our thinking, will be our retirement home. Being a few years away from retirement, I became preoccupied with this process. It was more than purchasing a home. My concern broadened to the implications of my age, the sense that I was nearing the end of my "active" ministry. How much consideration should we give to where our children were living in relation to where we might live? What would I do in retirement? How would I busy myself? What kind of ministry could I continue to perform? Was it wise to make this decision now? All of our savings would have to be poured into making the down payment.

For about six weeks, I could hardly get my mind off this monumental decision we were trying to make. That decision in a sense became my "dominant desire." *And that preoccupation did affect my praying.* Staying centered during my daily specific prayer times was difficult. I found myself unable to be as concerned about others as I normally am. I realized that, since this was my dominant desire, I had to surrender it completely to the Lord. And that wasn't easy. Only after days of deliberately laying this whole issue before the Lord in prayer was I free of my total preoccupation with it.

REFLECTING AND RECORDING

The following is a list of areas where our "dominant desire" often resides. We experience frustration and anxiety connected with these dimensions of life, and that experience seems to demand a lot of attention. In the space below each category, make some notes about how now, or at other times in your life, some issue connected with that area has been your dominant desire.

1. Family

2. Jobs and income

3. Age—the aging process or a stage of life

4. Security

DURING THE DAY

When you become preoccupied today with some "dominant desire," pray the Lord's Prayer.

DAY
3

A Continual State of Prayer

Pray without ceasing, give thanks in all circumstances; for this is the will of God in Christ Jesus for you.

—1 Thessalonians 5:17-18

Yesterday we considered prayer as *dominant desire.* What we desire most is our deepest prayer. Understood thus, prayer is reflected in our best thoughts and desires but also in our worst hours, our darkest thoughts and passions. For this reason we must intentionally flavor our daily lives with the conscious awareness of God's presence.

In Paul's instructions to the Thessalonians, he urged them to "pray without ceasing." Interestingly, these directions were given in the context of their belief in the imminent "second coming" of Christ. They were anxious and nervous about when the day of Christ's return would actually come. Jesus himself had told his followers that no one could know, that even he did not know; only God knows. That did not stop the speculation. In response, Paul told them the day would come suddenly and unexpectedly, and they needed to be ready. He advised them how they were to live in readiness. A part of his advice was "never stop praying"—*pray without ceasing.*

William Law offers a challenging case for praying without ceasing and a clear perception of our desires' being our true prayer. He discusses the value of different ways of praying and concludes, "If you would know what I would call a true and great gift of prayer, . . . it is a good heart, that stands continually inclined towards God."

Every man that has any feeling of the weight of his sin, or any true desire to be delivered from it by Christ, has learning and capacity enough to

make his own prayer. For praying is not speaking forth eloquently, but simply, the true desire of the heart; . . . the most simple souls, that have accustomed themselves to speak their own desires and wants to God, in such short, but true breathings of their hearts to him, will soon know more of prayer, and the mysteries of it, than any persons who have only their knowledge from learning, and learned books. . . .

It is not therefore silence, or a simple petition, or a great variety of outward expressions, that alters the nature of prayer, or makes it to be good, or better, but only and solely the reality, steadiness and continuity of the desire; and therefore whether a man offers this desire to God in the silent longing of the heart, or in simple short petitions, or in a great variety of words is of no consequence; . . . But if you would know what I would call a true and great gift of prayer, and what I most of all wish for myself, it is a good heart, that stands continually inclined towards God. (*Spirit of Prayer*, Pryr-2.3-48, Pryr-2.3-51, Pryr-2.3-52)

Law instructs us in two ways about praying without ceasing. First we must be aware of and acknowledge our sin. Read again Law's first paragraph.

❖   ❖   ❖

Law makes the case for our ability or capacity for prayer. I urge you to take that further in giving shape and content to unceasing prayer. We are not to be preoccupied with our sin, shame, and guilt, but prayer is not complete without confession of sin.

The second directive in Law's word is to be honest and open in expressing our wants and desires to the Lord. Our prayers are *unreal* and *ineffectual* because they do not truly represent what we deeply desire.

A young man for whom I once provided spiritual direction exemplifies a challenge many of us face. This young man had become a Christian only a few months before we began our conversations, converted in our church. He had begun attending initially because he married a church member. I discovered rather quickly that he was what I call a *prealcoholic*. All the signs of a growing addiction were present but not yet crippling enough to be obvious. I confronted him with the signs as I saw them. He acknowledged I might be right, and we began to pray about the issue. Though he was *earnest* and *passionate* in expressing his needs, a genuine reality in his praying was absent. He refused to give up the practice and relationships (the playmates and play-places) where his habit thrived.

To pray without ceasing does not mean we are satisfied simply to express our deepest desires as our ongoing prayer. Paul's call to pray without ceasing is a call to the disciplines of *intention* and *attention*. We must begin our day in prayer, bringing the whole of ourselves—body, mind, spirit—into God's presence. In that deliberate time and communion with God, we make it our *intention* to move through the day with God.

Attention is the discipline required for moving through the day with God. We have to be deliberately attentive to our relationship. The WWJD (What Would Jesus Do?) movement is an expression of this attentiveness. People wear WWJD bracelets or pins or put stickers in places to remind them to ask themselves, "What would Jesus do?" However we manage it, the discipline is essential: We are to attend to the presence of God and the implications of our relationship to Jesus for the whole of life.

REFLECTING AND RECORDING

The following prayer by W. E. Orchard expresses our need for the disciplines of intention and attention, the need for us to be aware of and acknowledge our sin, and to be honest in expressing our wants and desires to the Lord. After each paragraph there is a call for reflection. You may put the prayer into your own words in the space provided, a helpful exercise. Whether or not you write out your thoughts, spend enough time with each paragraph to make it your prayer.

O God, whose Spirit searches all things, and whose love bears all things, encourage us to draw near to Thee in sincerity and in truth. Save us from a worship of the lips while our hearts are far away. Save us from the useless labor of attempting to conceal ourselves from Thee who searches the heart.

Enable us to lay aside all those cloaks and disguises which we wear in the light of day and here to bare ourselves, with all our weakness, disease and sin, naked to Thy sight.

Make us strong enough to bear the vision of the truth, and to have done with all falsehood, pretense, and hypocrisy, so that we may see things as they are, and fear no more.

Enable us to look upon the love which has borne with us and the heart that suffers for us. Help us to acknowledge our dependence on the purity that abides our uncleanness, the patience that forgives our faithlessness, the truth that forbears all our falsity and compromise. And may we have the grace of gratitude, and the desire to dedicate ourselves to Thee. Amen. (W. E. Orchard, quoted in Fosdick, *Meaning of Prayer*, 134)

DURING THE DAY

There is a difference between learning the Lord's Prayer *by memory* and praying it *by heart*. With the notion of praying without ceasing, pray the Lord's Prayer *by heart* often today as a discipline of intention and attention.

DAY
4

The Soul Wholly Given to God

Protect me, O God, for in you I take refuge.
I say to the Lord, "You are my Lord;
    I have no good apart from you."

As for the holy ones in the land, they are the noble,
    in whom is all my delight.
Those who choose another god multiply their sorrows;
    their drink offerings of blood I will not pour out
    or take their names upon my lips.

The Lord is my chosen portion and my cup;
    you hold my lot.
The boundary lines have fallen for me in pleasant places;
    I have a goodly heritage.

I bless the Lord who gives me counsel;
    in the night also my heart instructs me.
I keep the Lord always before me;
    because he is at my right hand, I shall not be moved.

Therefore my heart is glad, and my soul rejoices;
    my body also rests secure.
For you do not give me up to Sheol,
    or let your faithful one see the Pit.

You show me the path of life.
    In your presence there is fullness of joy;
    in your right hand are pleasures forevermore.
                                                —Psalm 16

Some scholars believe that Psalm 16 was composed by a convert from one of the Canaanite peoples. This person, who was not a member of the covenant people of Israel, had found in Israel's faith in Yahweh, the Lord, what he had long hoped to be true. That God was indeed the Rock—which Israel said he was—became a reality (Knight, *Psalms,* 75–76).

The writer of Psalm 18, a Hebrew, refers to "my God, my rock, in whom I take refuge" (verse 2). The foreigner who writes in Psalm 16 has experienced God in the same way. Until now he has known God as a Supreme Being—which is the way he refers to God in verse 1. But beginning with verse 2 of Psalm 16, he addresses this Supreme Being as Lord, saying, "You are my Lord; I have no good apart from you." The writer has come to a newfound faith and a newfound relationship. He goes on to say that he has deliberately, and in complete freedom of choice, chosen Yahweh and found him to be all that he could long for.

George A. F. Knight reminds us that "the phrase *chosen portion* comes from the time when the land of Israel was being allotted amongst the twelve tribes of Israel. Each tribe then received [its] portion. His *cup* is just another way of saying the same thing. Obviously he can't help repeating himself with joy" (Knight, *Psalms,* 75–76). "The Lord is my chosen portion and my cup; you hold my lot" (verse 5). The height of this new convert's rejoicing is expressed in verse 9, "Therefore my heart is glad, and my soul rejoices; my body also rests secure." The whole of him—heart, soul, and body—rejoices.

The awareness of God as our rock, our refuge, is a critical part of prayer. Nothing brings me more deeply to this awareness than being on the beach, tuned to the Lord. Nothing is a more renewing tonic for my being—heart, soul, and body—than some time beside the ocean. The tingling sand beneath bare feet sends relaxing vibrations through my body, which get to my spirit also. The rhythmic swooshing of the waves seems to bring the different parts of my being into harmony, washing away weariness and anxiety. The wind freshens, invigorates, sometimes chills my body and, in an enlivening way, makes me conscious of the winds of the Spirit—sometimes calm, sometimes vigorous, sometimes chilling, sometimes fiery—sweeping through my soul. I seem to come alive on the beach.

Recently I observed two beach creatures who spoke to me. One I knew—the gull, the graceful soaring gull. The other I did not know so well—a sandpiper. The seagull spends most of its time in the air, sailing gracefully around, swooping up and down, and taking advantage of every wind shift. The sandpiper appeared rather clumsy by comparison. Now I know the good God made no mistake in creation, and I am sure the sandpiper lives out its potential in nature. Even so, comparing the gull and sandpiper provided a parable for my life.

The sandpiper scampers about on the beach, rather frantically looking for food. When the waves recede, the bird runs swiftly after the receding waters, laying hold of what little morsel of food may be left behind. Then the sandpiper retreats, either temporarily satisfied or empty-mouthed, to await another chance at the waste of the waves. I saw myself in the sandpiper—living by episodes, often frantic, never quite satisfied, missing the morsel as often as I find it. And strange to me, I observed that the sandpiper, while standing on the beach waiting for the next wave, stands on only one foot. Now that may be nature's best way for the sandpiper but not for us humans. Yet how often do I find myself standing on one foot, as it were, spiritually and emotionally, not even using the resources I know are available to me—neglecting the scriptures, casual in prayer, holding back from fellowship that could support me if I would take the initial risk.

How different the seagull appeared. At home and at ease—no appearance of anxiety or franticness. And though I would not want to press the analogy too far, the lesson was clear to me: I can be at home with my world and myself. I can relax and be in harmony. I can soar.

The Lord, knowing how fickle I am, and how much of me I read into everything I see, spoke to me that day saying, "Don't be too critical and analytical—just take what you see and try to apply it." Since I was working on this book and was immersing myself in some of the "saints," I remembered these words of William Law's:

The Poverty of our fallen Nature, the depraved Workings of Flesh and Blood, the corrupt Tempers of our polluted Birth in this World, do us no hurt, so long as the *Spirit of Prayer* works contrary to them, and longs for the first Birth of the Light and Spirit of Heaven.

All our natural Evil ceases to be our *own Evil* as soon as our Will-Spirit turns from it; it then changes its Nature, loses all its Poison and Death, and only becomes our *holy Cross*, on which we happily die from Self and this World into the Kingdom of Heaven. . . .

Reading is good, Hearing is good, Conversation and Meditation are good; but then they are only good at Times and Occasions . . ..

But the *Spirit of Prayer* is for all Times, and all Occasions; it is a Lamp that is to be always burning, a light to be ever shining, every Thing calls for it, every Thing is to be done in it, and governed by it; because it is and means, and wills nothing else, but the whole Totality of the Soul, not doing this or that, but wholly, incessantly given up to God to be *where*, and *what*, and *how* he pleases. (*Works*, IX:153, 157–58)

REFLECTING AND RECORDING

Read carefully each of Law's paragraphs above; get clearly in mind what he is saying, then write your own version beside each paragraph.

✤   ✤   ✤

DURING THE DAY

Continue praying the Lord's Prayer by heart as a discipline of intention and attention.

DAY
5

The Transforming Power of Prayer

My soul, wait silently for God alone,
For my expectation is from Him.
He only is my rock and my salvation;
He is my defense;
I shall not be moved.
In God is my salvation and my glory;
The rock of my strength,
And my refuge, is in God.

Trust in Him at all times, you people;
Pour out your heart before Him;
God is a refuge for us.
—Psalm 62:5-8, NKJV

One of my mentors in prayer was Douglas Steere. He was a brilliant man who taught philosophy at Haverford College for most of his professional life and wrote many books on prayer. The first of his books to get my attention when I was a young preacher was *Dimensions of Prayer*, written as a study book for the women of the Methodist Church but widely used among Christians in all denominations. I began to read everything he wrote: *Doors into Life, Time to Spare, On Beginning from Within, On Listening to Another, Work and Contemplation, Prayer and Worship,* and *Together in Solitude.*

I came to know him personally in the mid-1970s when he invited me to be a part of a group called the Ecumenical Institute of Spirituality, which he had founded following Vatican II. Eighteen to twenty-five people (the number varied through the years) from different denominations and faith perspectives—Roman Catholic, Protestant, Orthodox—came together once a year to share our spiritual pilgrimages. We would each share our autobiographical journey from the time we had last met. Then we would spend the rest of our time responding to a paper (or sometimes two) written by a member of the group. It was a rich and rewarding time of my life.

As a result of that group relationship, I had the wonderful opportunity of sharing a good bit of personal time with Douglas. I will never forget some days I spent in his home, which overlooked the wide expanse of Lake Michigan. It was a place of quiet and solitude. A hundred yards in back of the house in a kind of wooded area, he had built a study. That is where he did most of his praying and writing. He would go there early in the morning, usually about six o'clock, and spend at least an hour in prayer before breakfast. He invited me to join him there for that time.

There was little or no speaking during that hour—almost complete silence, opening ourselves to the Lord, listening to him. I have never been as proficient in that practice as I would like to be, and as I still seek to discipline myself to be, but I discovered in that experience the secret of who Douglas Steere was. He witnessed to it himself: that hour spent with the Lord, sharing intimate communion, shaped his soul.

We need to see prayer as a transforming power in our life. Teresa of Avila also witnessed to this dimension of prayer.

> **What great blessings God grants to a soul when He prepares it to love the practice of prayer, though it may not be as well prepared already as it should be; and how, if that soul perseveres, notwithstanding the sins, temptations and falls of a thousand kinds in to which the devil leads it, the Lord, I am certain, will bring it to the harbour of salvation, just as, so far as can at present be told, He has brought me. May His Majesty grant that I may never again be lost.**
>
> **The blessings possessed by one who practises prayer—I mean mental prayer—have been written of by many saints and good men. Glory be to God for this . . . no one who has begun this practice, however many sins he may commit, should ever forsake it. For it is the means by which we may amend our lives again, and without it amendment will be very much harder . . . . And anyone who has not begun to pray, I beg, for love of the Lord, not to miss so great a blessing.** (*Complete Works of Saint Teresa*, I:49-50)

Teresa uses a vivid phrase to picture this transforming power of prayer: "the harbour of salvation." Sins, temptations, and relapses "of a thousand kinds" are overcome through prayer. This affirmation supports my observation that prayer made Douglas Steere the great soul he was. Steere witnessed to it himself way back in 1938 when he wrote, "It does not matter where or with what petitions we begin in prayer. *What is really important is where we end, where we are brought to in prayer.* The real question to ask of ourselves after prayer is: 'Were you faithful? Did you yield?'" (Steere, *Prayer and Worship*, 29)

For the past three years, I have been using prayer to transform my impatience. Through the years of my public life, I have suppressed outward signs of impatience—

and became quite masterful at it. Inside, the churning was torrential. It not only kept me "on edge," it affected negatively my focused thinking and sleep. I don't know why I had not made this a concentrated issue of prayer earlier. Of course I had prayed for the Lord to give me patience, but I had not made that a *dominant desire*, which we considered on Day Two of this week. I continued to limit, even completely disallow, any outward expression of my boiling inside. During these years of using prayer in a deliberate way to transform my impatience, I have done primarily two things. One, I have honestly confessed my impatience to the Lord. Two, I have used psalms like the one quoted above to calm the churning within and give perspective.

REFLECTING AND RECORDING

Recall and record here an experience of the transforming power of prayer in your own life.

If your personal journey has not yet yielded such an identifiable experience, try to think of someone whose journey has been marked by such an experience and spend some time thinking about that individual.

✦ ✦ ✦

Read again the last three sentences of the text from Teresa above.

✦ ✦ ✦

Read again the psalm for today.

✦ ✦ ✦

Now write a brief prayer, reflecting the psalmist's feeling.

DURING THE DAY

Seek out someone whom you can ask how prayer has transformed his or her life. Continue to pray by heart the Lord's Prayer.

DAY
6

The Prayer of the Heart

The Asbury Seminary library includes the Carver Healing Collection, a collection of materials, letters, audiotapes, books, movies, tracts, and advertisements related to the healing revival from 1955 to 1994. It is a remarkable documentation of one of the most significant phenomena in recent American religious history. We had the formal opening of that collection on the weekend of April 17, 1999. As a part of that celebration, we showed the film entitled "Raise the Dead." This film, produced and directed for public television by James Rutenbeck, chronicles the ministry of healing evangelism in Appalachia, especially that of Brother H. Richard Hall.

James Rutenbeck was with us to celebrate and to lead a forum in response to the film. Following this event, I wrote him a letter expressing my appreciation for his contribution to our understanding of a healing revival that has been a unique aspect of the religious landscape in the second half of the twentieth century. In response to my letter, he wrote:

Making this film has taken me to unexpected places—both geographically and spiritually. When we first started out in 1993, my son Anthony was three and showing the first signs of a developmental disorder which even now prevents him from speaking. After years of agnosticism, I began to pray for him. That, coupled with the long process of making the film, has changed me.

Like characters out of Flannery O'Connor, Brothers Hall, Ferree and Sister Shelton are extreme in their expression of faith. In some ways though, I think the sheer audacity of their vision is what was required to reach someone like me. That and a child in need. I can't say I believe divine healing is something I could ever lean on, but I do finally understand what it means to find solace in prayer and perhaps a kind of healing for myself.

Well, I've said more than I expected, but I hope you understand. I tell you this not to burden you but because I like you and somehow feel you will understand.

When I received that letter I immediately thought of a portion of Psalm 145:

> The LORD is just in all his ways,
>   and kind in all his doings.
> The LORD is near to all who call on him,
>   to all who call on him in truth.
> He fulfills the desire of all who fear him;
>   he also hears their cry, and saves them.
> The LORD watches over all who love him,
>   but all the wicked he will destroy.
> —Psalm 145:17-20

I am not sure James knows that psalm, but he expressed the same deep conviction of the psalmist: "The Lord is near to all who call upon him . . . He fulfills the desire of all who fear him . . . He hears their cry, and saves them." This passage from William Law also speaks to the power of prayer.

> All outward power that we exercise in the things about us is but as a shadow in comparison of that inward power that resides in our will, imagination, and desires; these communicate with eternity and kindle a life which always reaches either heaven or hell. . . .
>
> Our desire is not only thus powerful and productive of real effects, but it is always alive, always working and creating in us. I say creating, for it has no less power, it perpetually generates either life or death in us.
>
> And here lies the ground of the great efficacy of prayer, which when it is the prayer of the heart, the prayer of faith, has a kindling and creating power, and forms and transforms the soul into every thing that its desires reach after.
>
> It has the key to the Kingdom of Heaven, and unlocks all its treasures, it opens, extends, and moves that in us which has its being and motion in and with the divine nature, and so brings us into real union and communion with God. (*Christian Devotion*, 85–86)

James's testimony confirms Law's teaching. As an agnostic, James began to pray. Providentially, he was involved in making a film that dealt with healing prayer, and it changed him. He is honest in what he affirms: "I can't say I believe divine healing is something I could ever lean on, but I do finally understand what it means to find solace in prayer and perhaps a kind of healing for myself."

Prayer is powerful and productive, as William Law affirms, and works in our life at different levels. In ways that we don't understand, it often brings healing to those for whom we pray. Even when such complete healing does not come, as was the case with Anthony, James Rutenbeck's son, still a creating power is kindled within us, which "forms and transforms the soul into every thing that its desires reach after."

REFLECTING AND RECORDING

Spend some time probing the depths of the following affirmations made by William Law:

> All outward power that we exercise in the things about us is but as a shadow in comparison of that inward power that resides in our will, imagination, and desires.

✠ ✠ ✠

> Our desire is not only thus powerful and productive of real effects, but it is always alive, always working and creating in us.

✠ ✠ ✠

> [Prayer] opens, extends, and moves that in us which has its being and motion in and with the divine nature, and so brings us into real union and communion with God.

✠ ✠ ✠

Recall and record some experience when your will, imagination, or desires shaped powerful results in your praying. Write enough to make that remembered experience come alive.

DURING THE DAY

Did you ask a person yesterday to tell you how prayer has transformed his or her life? Do the same today—talk to another person. Look for an opportunity to share with someone the experience you wrote about above.

DAY
7

When We Are Honest, Healing Begins

Trust in the LORD, and do good;
Dwell in the land, and feed on His faithfulness.
Delight yourself also in the LORD,
And He shall give you the desires of your heart.

Commit your way to the LORD,
Trust also in Him,
And He shall bring it to pass.
He shall bring forth your righteousness as the light,
And your justice as the noonday.

—Psalm 37:3-6, NKJV

The righteous cry out, and the LORD hears,
And delivers them out of all their troubles.
The LORD is near to those who have a broken heart,
And saves such as have a contrite spirit.
Many are the afflictions of the righteous,
But the LORD delivers him out of them all.

—Psalm 34:17-19, NKJV

Our seminary community is a praying community. In September of 1998, as we began our school year, one of our students, Tanya Woodham, and her fiancé, Daryl, were in an accident. Daryl was killed; Tanya was injured and near death. She was hospitalized for weeks and in intense physical therapy after that. She returned to school and graduated in May 1999.

Two weeks before commencement day, we have Graduates Week at the seminary, with three chapel services. Our graduating students preach, and in each service there are two testimonies. In one of these services, Tanya gave her testimony. This is what she said:

I came here three years ago to learn how to be a Christian counselor that I might help others. I had no idea what God would teach me. The last nine months have been my greatest teachers. It hasn't been through a classroom lecture, a book, or a paper. It has been through life experience. In case there are those of you who aren't aware, nine months ago I was involved in a car accident that almost took my life and did take the life of my fiancé, Daryl.

As I struggled with what to say this morning, God told me that my life was a testimony of his grace. Everyone could see the miracle God performed on my body. Instead God wanted me to tell you about my heart and spirit. The following prayer is one that I believe God wants me to share with you.

Lord, you told me if I delighted myself in You, You would give me the desires of my heart (Ps. 37:4). Then why is my heart broken?

Lord, you told me that you would be near to those who have a broken heart and a contrite spirit (Ps. 34:18). Then why do I feel so alone? . . .

Life seems unfair and all I can do is ask, "Why?" . . .

I've been told that your ways are not my ways and your thoughts are not my thoughts (Isa. 55:8).

I've been told that all things work for good (Rom. 8:28). . . .

But how can I trust when you allowed these struggles which have broken my heart in two?

It is so hard to trust.

But as I continue to look at Jesus' life, I feel especially drawn to him.

I feel that I understand some small piece of what suffering is all about and how much he must have really loved me.

And even though it is hard to trust and I'm sad and I'm angry, I know deep within me that one day my trust in God the Father will return greater than it was nine months ago. I long for that day when my faith under fire will be the strongest it has ever been.

But until then, I am unable to carry myself.

I need for you and your servants to have the trust for me.

As a Christian, it was very hard for me to admit that I was angry and disappointed in God and to ask a sovereign God "Why?" But I heard God whisper, "Just be honest with me. Talk to me and tell me how you really feel." It is when we are honest that healing begins. Thank you as a community for praying for my healing, supporting me, and encouraging me to be honest with God.

No one can prescribe the direction your praying should take. But pray we must, whatever the circumstance and however we express ourselves. As we have said, honesty is a key to effective praying. In her testimony, Tanya not only responded to

God's leading for her own soul's sake; she inspired and taught her classmates. It would have been natural to talk of God's miraculous healing of her body. We expected that. She could have done so, and we would have never known the pain and struggle within her heart. Julian of Norwich is right. One purpose of prayer is "to make the soul willing and responsive to God."

> For when a soul is tempted, troubled and left to herself in her unrest, that is the time for her to pray and to make herself supple and obedient to God. But he by no kind of prayer makes God supple to him; for God's love does not change. And so I saw that when we see the need for us to pray, then our Lord God is following us, helping our desire. And when we by his special grace behold him plainly, seeing no other, we then necessarily follow him, and he draws us to him by love. For I saw and felt that his wonderful and total goodness fulfils all our powers; and with that I saw that his continual working in every kind of thing is done so divinely, so wisely and so powerfully that it surpasses all our imagining and everything that we can understand or think. (*Showings*, 254–55)

REFLECTING AND RECORDING

Recall and record briefly an occasion when your questions *to* God were far more intense than your faith *in* God.

Read again Julian's words above. Does Tanya's experience or the outcome of the experience you recorded above verify Julian's claim?

✦ ✦ ✦

DURING THE DAY

In the group with which you are sharing this workbook journey is anyone going through a time of testing and questioning? If so, pray for that person now and throughout the day.

Group Meeting
for Week Four

INTRODUCTION

Paul advised the Philippians to "let your conversation be as it becometh the gospel of Christ" (Phil. 1:27, KJV). Most of us may not have yet seen the dynamic potential of the kind conversation to which Paul calls the Philippians. Life is found in communion with God and also in conversation with others.

Speaking and listening with the sort of deep meaning that communicates life is not easy. All of us have experiences that are not easy to talk about. Therefore, listening and responding to what we hear is important. To really hear another person helps him or her to think clearly and gain perspective. To listen, then, is an act of love. When we listen to another, we say, "I value you. You are important." When we listen in a way that makes a difference, we surrender ourselves to the other, saying, "I will hear what you have to say and will receive you as I receive your words." When we speak in a way that makes a difference, we speak for the sake of others; thus we are contributing to their understanding and wholeness.

1. Ask the group if anyone would like to share something special that has happened during the past week or two, connected with his or her use of this workbook.

2. Did anyone have an experience with the Lord's Prayer he or she would like to share?

3. Ask the group members to turn in their workbooks to the Reflecting and Recording section of Day One. Read aloud Teresa's one-sentence claim and invite those who are willing to read their *version* of this sentence.

4. Now spend five to eight minutes discussing the notion that the more we humble ourselves in prayer, the more God lifts us up.

5. Invite two or three members to share an experience when they were overwhelmed by Christ's presence and did not feel worthy to be there (Reflecting and Recording, Day One.)

6. The theme of Day Two was *prayer as dominant desire*. In the Reflecting and Recording section are four areas in which we often experience frustration and anxiety. Ask group members to share experiences in each area when particular issues became dominant desires in their prayer life.

7. Spend eight to ten minutes discussing this claim: "To pray without ceasing does not mean we are satisfied simply to express our deepest desires as our ongoing prayer. Paul's call to pray without ceasing is a call to the disciplines of *intention* and *attention*."

8. Invite two or three participants to share an experience of the transforming power of prayer in their lives.

9. In your remaining time, discuss Law's statement in the Reflecting and Recording section of Day Six. Concentrate on each affirmation in turn.

Praying Together

1. Begin your prayer time by having someone read the last two paragraphs of William Law's text at the close of Day Four. Ask another volunteer to read his or her version of those two paragraphs.

2. Invite someone to pray a revision of W. E. Orchard's prayer on Day Three.

3. Corporate prayer is one of the great blessings of Christian community. I invite you to go deeper now, experimenting with the possibilities of corporate prayer by sharing in the fashion described here.

    Bow in silence and in prayerful concern. The leader calls the name of a person in the group, and someone else in the group offers a brief prayer for the individual named. Then the leader calls another name, and that person is prayed for. The prayers may be brief—two or three sentences—or longer. Think of the person whose name is called. What concern or need has she shared tonight or in the past weeks that could be mentioned in prayer? You may want to express gratitude for the person's life and witness, the role he is playing in the group, or her ministry in the community. Someone may be seeking direction or need to make a crucial decision. Let someone pray for each individual in a particular way.

Love

The Highest Gift
of God

DAY
1

"My Worst Could Not Destroy Their Love for Me"

Her name was Diane. The Very Reverend Nathan D. Baxter tells her story.

Diane grew up in a good and loving home. There were family outings, birthday celebrations, softball, dance classes and even church. But for some reason Diane never felt quite OK, and somewhere in high school things went awry. There was smoking, drugs, stealing, alcohol, staying out late.

The family suffered social embarrassment and seemed increasingly in crisis—trying to reach out to Diane, while also struggling to maintain the family's life and values. There was counseling, rehabilitation, tough love, tears and prayers. But the more they reached out to her, the more abusive and rebellious she became. Finally, she ran away, living a life she'd rather not talk about. She was well in her mid-to-late-twenties before healing and reconciliation began.

Diane said, "At first, I felt my parents' love was unnecessary. It was smothering. Then as things got worse, I began to feel unlovable. I think I resented my parents most because if I was unlovable I could do what I wanted and it would not matter. But as long as I suspected I was loved I wasn't free 'to do my thing.' So I needed to destroy their love in order for me to be free.

"But," she said, "they never stopped loving me. Even when I got arrested and they refused to bail me out of jail, I could see the pain of love in their eyes. Now I realize how much I have needed their love and prayers that kept me alive all these years. But when I look back on those years, what amazes me most of all is that my worst could not destroy their love for me."

That last word is a telling one. As our divine parent, God's love of us never ends. It is like a parent's love for a prodigal child. Even if we reject God, God will never reject us. The Old Testament prophet Hosea makes this case dramatically, as he reports God saying:

When Israel was a child, I loved him,
  and out of Egypt I called my son.
The more I called them,
  the more they went from me;
they kept sacrificing to the Baals,
  and offering incense to idols.

Yet it was I who taught Ephraim to walk,
  I took them up in my arms;
  but they did not know that I healed them.
I led them with cords of human kindness,
  with bands of love.
I was to them like those
  who lift infants to their cheeks.
I bent down to them and fed them.
                    —Hosea 11:1-4

Earlier, in chapters 1 and 2 of his book, Hosea compares the relationship of God and Israel to that of husband and wife. Israel was like a wife who ran away from her husband. Under the law, the husband had a right to get rid of her, and most husbands would do that. Hosea uses his own marriage to Gomer to make his point. Gomer had forsaken him and was living as a prostitute. Eventually Hosea found her in a slave market—she had sunk so low—and he bought her back. He says God acts like that. Symbolically, God is married to Israel. Israel, like Gomer, had run away to worship other gods, but God has bought her back.

Hosea insists that God will not abandon Israel. God is faithful, has given a promise, and will keep that promise. After using the metaphor of God as a spouse, faithful even though the partner in the marriage is unfaithful, Hosea changes the metaphor to God as parent in chapter 11. God could be either a father or a mother, because the feelings here are parental feelings. God carries on a kind of monologue, talking about what to do with a child, torn between the behavior of the child and the feelings that only a parent can have. "When Israel was a child, I loved him . . . the more I called him, the more they went from me . . . yet it was I who taught Ephraim to walk; I took them up in my arms . . . but they did not know that I healed them . . . I loved them with cords of human kindness, with bands of love. . . ." Later in chapter 11, God says, "I will not execute my fierce, fierce anger . . . for I am God and no mortal, the Holy One in your midst, and I will not come in wrath" (verse 9). It is a picture of a God whose love never ends, who will never reject us even though we reject God. This love is the heart of the Christian faith.

Love is a primary theme of many spiritual writers. All the saints with whom we are keeping company on this workbook journey consider love a core principle. William Law states the case this way:

All religion is the spirit of Love; all its gifts and graces are the gifts and graces of love; it has no breath, no life, but the life of love. Nothing exalts, nothing purifies, but the fire of love; nothing changes death into life, earth into heaven, [mortals] into angels, but love alone. Love breathes the Spirit of God; its words and works are the inspiration of God. Love speaketh not of itself, but the Word, the eternal Word of God speaketh in it; for all that love speaketh, that God speaketh, because love is God. Love is heaven revealed in the soul; it is light, and truth; it is infallible; it has no errors, for all errors are the want of love. Love has no more of pride, than light has of darkness; it stands and bears all its fruits from a depth, and root of humility. Love is of no sect or party; it neither makes, nor admits of any bounds; you may as easily enclose the light or shut up the air of the world in one place, as confine love to a sect or party. It lives in the liberty, the universality, the impartiality of heaven. (*Spirit of Prayer*, Pryr-2.3-9)

REFLECTING AND RECORDING

Ponder some of Law's radical claims about love.

"Nothing purifies, but the fire of love." Spend some time thinking about how something gone wrong in your life was made right by love.

❖ ❖ ❖

"Nothing changes death into life, . . . but love alone." Have you had a relationship that was dead or nearly destroyed by your action and attitude and was brought to life again by love? (Or do you know of another person's experience of love's transforming power?)

❖ ❖ ❖

Can you think of a marriage relationship that might have been destroyed because of unfaithfulness on one partner's part but was kept alive by the loving faithfulness of the other?

❖ ❖ ❖

"Nothing changes . . . earth into heaven, [mortals] into angels, but love alone." Think about all the ways your life—relationships, circumstances, goals, directions, values—have been transformed by love.

❖ ❖ ❖

DURING THE DAY

The following word from William Law is printed on page 203. Cut it and put it in a place where you will see it often during the day. Let the truth of it determine your actions and attitudes during the day. "Love has no more of pride than light has of darkness; it stands and bears all its fruits from a depth, and root of humility."

DAY

2

"You Will Always Be My Dad"

We are debtors—not to the flesh, to live according to the flesh. For if you live according to the flesh you will die; but if by the Spirit you put to death the deeds of the body, you will live. For as many as are led by the Spirit of God, these are sons [and daughters] of God. For you did not receive the spirit of bondage again to fear, but you received the Spirit of adoption by whom we cry out, "Abba, Father." The Spirit . . . bears witness with our spirit that we are children of God, and if children, their heirs—heirs of God and joint heirs with Christ, if indeed we suffer with Him, that we may also be glorified together.

—Romans 8:12–17, NKJV

Paul must have known, perhaps through Luke or Mark, that Jesus called God "Abba." Mark recorded in his Gospel that in Gethsemane, when the cross was looming ahead, Jesus prayed "Abba, Father, for you all things are possible; remove this cup from me; yet, not what I want, but what you want" (Mark 14:36). Not only in the Romans passage quoted above, but also in his Epistle to the Galatians, Paul designates us as children who use that affectionate, intimate address to God—"Abba, Daddy." "And because you are children, God has sent the Spirit of his Son into our hearts, crying, 'Abba, Father!'" (Gal. 4:6)

It's not easy to grasp the notion—especially for people who have not had a good, loving, affirming, earthly father. Once in a teaching conference, I confessed my feelings of some failure as a dad with my son, Kevin. A woman in the audience picked up on my honesty and willingness to be vulnerable. She wrote me a letter, in which she said:

> When I heard you boldly speak of your need to come to terms with your own imperfect fathering, my heart broke in response. . . . Three hours ago we were talking at the service and I had so much more I needed to say so I felt I needed to write to my Dad who died five years ago at ninety-one—a grand pioneer missionary doctor in Africa. He died with only five days' warning of advanced leukemia . . . he had been actively serving God right up to the end.

She sent a copy of the letter she had written to her deceased father. A portion of it read:

> The intensity of my anger still frightens me. As a child I didn't know how to tell you how angry I was because I love you so. The scary, stiff, Victorian image of Father God who needed my perfect obedience without talking back led me to stuff my fears of being alone and so I had to work out my struggles on my own; always trying to pull from God His wisdom as a reward for being good. I have spent most of my life being busy for you and now that I am almost fifty I'm discovering how good it is to get angry, to cry a whole lot, to discover the tidal pull of life's cycles of pain and joy. Life is so much more real now and it amazes me to watch how my capacity to get close to others has radically changed. The spiky quills of fear are dissolving in this mysterious alchemy of truth inside my heart. It is hard to recognize that the God of the evangelical church still reflects a demanding external compliance to rules and work and ways of loving. I have longed, Dad, to talk this out with you or the local church fathers, but they still appear to be too busy to take the time to listen; they are still moving along with all their programs for change. Some of our mothers are quietly listening in the solitude of their hearts but they are still finding their voice and their courage to tell their story, just like me. So I find that my analyst does the best job of helping me find God in my life and she isn't a "believer" . . . at least not how we term it. I wonder what God thinks. Do I make you sad, Dad? Can you grieve with me? I hope you are listening.
>
> These past years, much to my surprise, I am finding that I grow stronger living out all my questions. Life is full of these paradoxes. They leave me gasping for air as I come up to the surface from my depth encounters with the Divine in me, so I guess this letter is just a start to open a dialogue today that has been a long time coming and I have not had the words to speak before. Can we learn to let go and forgive together? I have a strange hope in my heart today. God is here with you and me, even in our separateness and

distance. My longing for you feels like an emotional tsunami but I know you can help calm my panic-driven anxieties. After all you will ALWAYS be my Dad!

Accept the rough tumblings of my soul; they come with deeper affection and love than I have ever felt before.

Your precious loved child,————.

You can feel the intensity, the anguish, the pain, the retching up of grievances that can't be handled in person, face to face. The feelings are so deep that she has a compulsion to put words on paper, to write to a father who will never read the words from the page stained with tears.

We are fortunate if we have had a father who can demonstrate, in his relationship to us, even faintly what our heavenly Father is like. Though helpful, that experience is not essential to knowing God. We are not to judge God by the character of our own earthly father but to know that our heavenly Father is like the father who welcomed the prodigal son home and threw an extravagant party, like the shepherd who left ninety-nine sheep and risked himself searching for the one that was lost.

While spiritual writers talk about God as Spirit, dwelling within and dwelling everywhere, they sometimes give that Spirit the name of Father. Teresa of Avila did this in teaching about prayer:

> You know that God is everywhere, which is a great truth; wherever God dwells there is heaven, and you may feel sure that all which is glorious is near His Majesty.
>
> Remember what St. Augustine tells us—I think it comes in his Meditations; how he sought God in many places and at last found the Almighty within himself. Do you consider it of slight importance for a soul given to wandering thoughts to realize this truth and to see that it has no need to go to heaven in order to speak to the eternal Father or to enjoy His company? Nor is it requisite to raise the voice to address Him, for He hears every whisper however low.
>
> We are not forced to take wings to find Him, but have only to seek solitude and to look within ourselves.
>
> Address Him sometimes as Father, or as Brother, or again as a Master or as your Bridegroom: sometimes in one way, sometimes in another, He will teach you what He wishes you to do. (*Living Water*, 32)

REFLECTING AND RECORDING

List three or four of the most common ways you address God in prayer:

1.

2.

3.

4.

List three or four titles for God that you may have difficulty using or that simply are not common ways you address God in your praying.

1.

2.

3.

4.

Spend a bit of time thinking about the experiences of your life—relationships, corporate worship, family, private devotions—that have determined how you address God.

❖   ❖   ❖

How has Teresa's following statement been verified, or how does it need to be verified, in your life? "We are not forced to take wings to find Him, but have only to seek solitude and to look within ourselves."

❖   ❖   ❖

DURING THE DAY

Continue reflecting on the maxim by William Law that you clipped yesterday, letting the truth of it determine your actions1 and attitudes.

D A Y
3

His Mark Is Upon Us

"All things are lawful," but not all things are beneficial. "All things are lawful," but not all things build up. Do not seek your own advantage, but that of the other. Eat whatever is sold in the meat market without raising any question on the ground of conscience, for "the earth and its fullness are the Lord's." If an unbeliever invites you to a meal and you are disposed to go, eat whatever is set before you without raising any question on the ground of conscience. But if someone says to you, "This has been offered in sacrifice," then do not eat it, out of consideration for the one who informed you, and for the sake of conscience—I mean the other's conscience, not your own. For why should my liberty be subject to the judgment of someone else's conscience? If I partake with thankfulness, why should I be denounced because of that for which I give thanks? So, whether you eat or drink, or whatever you do, do everything for the glory of God. Give no offense to Jews or to Greeks or to the church of God, just as I try to please everyone in everything I do, not seeking my own advantage, but that of many, so that they may be saved.

—1 Corinthians 10:23-33

These are the closing verses of chapter 10 of 1 Corinthians. But verse 1 of chapter 11 should be added because it is the conclusion of this part of Paul's discussion. "Be imitators of me, as I am of Christ." Is there some arrogance here? How many of us would call people to imitate us? The NIV translation softens it a bit: "Follow my example, as I follow the example of Christ."

Paul was probably the first Christian the Corinthians had met. They must have been intrigued to meet a man who was so certain of his faith, so confident of his relationship to God. There was the added attraction that he was not seeking personal advantage but was determined "to please everyone in everything I do, not seeking my own advantage, but that of many, so that they may be saved" (verse 33). His only concern was to introduce people to Christ and all the blessings faith and love provide. Of course, some of his people were more than willing to misjudge him (see

1 Cor. 4:3-4) or to challenge his leadership (2 Cor. 10:10), but his integrity was never seriously doubted.

As to the issue of arrogance, common sense says that those Christians in Corinth needed a role model. Who was better equipped to be that model than Paul? In thought, obedience, sacrifice, and love, he was a worthy example. There was no better evangelist, no more devoted pastor, for them to imitate. Even so, the key to the lesson is Paul's advice that they imitate *him as he imitated Christ*. Paul offered himself as a model insofar as he was following Christ.

In his letter to the Ephesians, Paul calls more boldly for imitation. "Therefore be imitators of God." How could this be—"imitators of God"? God is omnipotent. How could we imitate the One who is omnipotent—all-powerful? Omniscient—all-knowing? Omnipresent—present throughout creation and among all humankind? How can we imitate such a God?

Don't forget the incarnation. The Holy God became flesh. Born in the outbuilding of a little village inn to unimportant parents in an outback corner of the Roman Empire, Jesus was born of a people who were oppressed politically and depressed spiritually. He lived in virtual obscurity for thirty years, not in the capital city of Jerusalem but in the redneck town of Nazareth. His first sermon was in his home synagogue in Nazareth, where his own people and family rejected him. He healed unnamed people like Simon's mother-in-law, spent time with women, tax collectors, prostitutes, and sinners, and put his trust in a number of disciples who failed him at every point. He didn't separate himself from the world but touched lepers, allowed a sinful woman to anoint his feet, washed the disciples' feet, and wept with compassion over Jerusalem. In the end, he endured mocking, rejection, derision, ridicule, cruelty, pain, violence, and a torturous crucifixion.

This is the Holy God. So what does it mean to imitate God? It means to do what God has done in God's coming to us in Jesus Christ. Paul talks about that in these verses in which he calls us to imitate God: "Therefore be imitators of God as beloved children. And live in love, as Christ loved us and gave himself up for us, a fragrant offering and a sacrifice to God" (Eph. 5:1-2).

Christ is our pattern for holy living, for imitating God—and the pattern is "walk in love." All the great spiritual writers would agree with this notion of imitation, or copying. William Law wrote about it in this fashion:

God created everything to partake of his own nature, to have some degree and share of his own life and happiness. Nothing can be good or evil, happy or unhappy, but as it does or does not stand in the same degree of divine life in which it was created,

receiving in God and from God all that good that it is capable of, and cooperating with him according to the nature of its powers and perfections.

As soon as it turns to itself and would, as it were, have a sound of its own, it breaks off from the divine harmony and falls into the misery of its own discord; and all its workings then are only so many sorts of torment or ways of feeling its own poverty.

The redemption of mankind then can only be effected, the harmony of the creation can then only be restored when the will of God is the will of every creature. (*Joy of the Saints*, 76)

Have you seen the TV program *Antiques Road Show*? I seldom have the opportunity to watch it, but it intrigues me. It is good entertainment—and to some degree, educational. The show presents a group of appraisers who travel around the country and set up business at convention centers and/or civic auditoriums. They invite people to bring their antiques for appraisal. Someone will bring an old clock, a painting, a vase, a piece of furniture—something that may have been found in the attic or bought at a swap meet. The conversation between the appraiser and the owner of the object is really the interesting part of the show. The appraiser will ask the owner about the history of the object—where it came from, who bought it, how much was paid for it, if it were inherited—gathering some of the family history.

Then the appraiser will talk about the object and what he or she knows about it—the artist or designer, the date it was created, and the general market value when it was created. The dramatic moment comes the appraiser reveals what the object is worth at auction today. Some appraisals are amazing: a table that had been in the attic of one house for over fifty years was worth $75,000; a sword that was hidden away in a trunk was worth $110,000. And on and on it goes—making you want to go to your attic and see what you can find. To me, the most fascinating part of the program is when the appraiser shows the owner some hallmark, some special mark or signature or a date etched on the object. Such details allow the appraiser to reveal information you have never dreamed of. The bottom line is that the value of the object often is determined by the marks that are upon it.

William Law makes that very point when he talks about God's creating everything to *partake of God's own nature*. We stand in the same degree of divine life in which we are created, "receiving in God and from God all that good is capable of, and cooperating with [God] according to the nature of [our] powers and perfections." And that is what Paul is urging the Corinthians to do when he calls them to imitate him as he seeks to imitate Christ and also when he calls us to imitate God. Again William Law speaks to us.

> For this reason our blessed Lord, having taken upon him a created nature, so continually declares against the doing of anything of himself and always appeals to the will of God as the only motive and end of everything he did, saying that it was his meat and drink to do the will of him that sent him. (*Joy of the Saints*, 76)

REFLECTING AND RECORDING

In the space provided to the right of the quotation, paraphrase what Law says in the first paragraph on page 131.

✦   ✦   ✦

Now spend a few minutes reflecting on what it means to "partake of [God's] own nature."

✦   ✦   ✦

Thinking of the call upon you to imitate God, what are significant dimensions of God's character that you are missing? List two or three of your most glaring areas of deficiency.

DURING THE DAY

Continue reflecting on Law's maxim, which you clipped on Day One, letting the truth of it determine your actions and attitudes.

DAY
4

Do You Know Who You Are?

For just as the body is one and has many members, and all the members of the body, though many, are one body, so it is with Christ. For in the one Spirit we were all baptized into one body—Jews or Greeks, slaves or free—and we were all made to drink of one Spirit. Indeed, the body does not consist of one member but of many. If the foot would say, "Because I am not a hand, I do not belong to the body," that would not make it any less a part of the body. And if the ear would say," Because I am not an eye, I do not belong to the body," that would not make it any less a part of the body. If the whole body were an eye, where would the hearing be? But as it is, God arranged the members in the body, each one of them, as he chose. If all were a single member, where would the body be? As it is, there are many members, yet one body. The eye cannot say to the hand, "I have no need of you," nor again the head to feet, "I have no need of you." On the contrary, the members of the body that seem to be weaker are indispensable, and those members of the body that we think less honorable we clothe with greater honor, and our less respectable members are treated with greater respect; whereas our more respectable members do not need this. But God has so arranged the body, giving the greater honor to the inferior member, that there may be no dissension within the body, but the members may have the same care for one another. If one member suffers, all suffer together with it; if one member is honored, all rejoice together with it.

—1 Corinthians 12:12-26

Edwina Gately, who works with homeless and abused women, told this story:

Once upon a time there was a country ruled by a king. The country was invaded and the king was killed but his children were rescued by servants and hidden away. The smallest, an infant daughter, was reared by a peasant family. They didn't know she was the king's daughter. She had become the peasant's daughter, and she dug potatoes and lived in poverty.

One day an old woman came out of the forest and approached the young woman who was digging potatoes. The old woman asked her: "Do you know who you are?" And the young woman said, "Yes, I'm a farmer's daughter and a potato digger." The old woman said: "No, no, you are the daughter of the king." And the potato digger said: "I'm the daughter of the king?" "Yes, that's who you are!" And the old woman disappeared back into the forest.

After the old woman left, the young woman still dug potatoes but she dug them differently. It was the way she held her shoulders and it was the light in her eyes because she knew who she was. She knew she was the daughter of the king. (Wicks, *Seeds of Sensitivity*, 7)

Is anything more important than to know who we are? We are daughters and sons of God. Our salvation has been purchased by his love, in the gift of his Son, on the cross. Paul uses the image of adoption to describe what Christ has done for us:

But when the fullness of the time had come, God sent forth his Son, born of a woman, born under the law, in order to redeem those who were under the law, so that we might receive the adoption as children.

—Galatians 4:4-5

This means we are equally loved and accepted by God—thus, equally precious in God's sight. Teresa of Avila has a wonderful reflection on this truth:

It is important to understand that God doesn't lead all by one path . . . Saint Martha was a saint, even though they do not say she was contemplative. Well now, what more do you want than to be able to resemble this blessed woman who merited so often to have Christ our Lord in her home, give Him food, serve Him and eat at table with Him? If she had been enraptured like the Magdalene, there wouldn't have been anyone to give food to the divine Guest. Well, think of this congregation as the home of Saint Martha and that there must be people for every task. . . . [I]t is necessary for someone to prepare His meal and let them consider themselves lucky to serve with Martha. Let them consider how true humility consists very much in great readiness to be content with whatever the Lord may want to do with them and in always finding oneself unworthy to be called His servant. If contemplating, practicing mental and vocal prayer, taking care of the sick, helping with household chores, and working even at the lowliest tasks are all ways of serving the Guest who comes to be with us and eat and recreate, what difference does it make whether we serve in the one way or the other? (*Soul's Passion for God*, 31, 33–34)

Without this kind of reflection, we usually think Martha's sister, Mary, is the more favored one. In Luke's story (Luke 10:38-41), Jesus comes to the home of

Mary and Martha. Martha complains that instead of helping her in the kitchen, Mary is sitting at Jesus' feet, listening to him teach. Jesus gives this perspective: "Martha, Martha, you are worried and troubled about many things; there is need of only one thing. Mary has chosen the better part, which will not be taken away from her" (Luke 10:41-42).

Even so—though Martha may have been too distracted from "the better way" by her work, we still need Martha. In the Corinthians passage with which we began today, Paul images the church as a body with each member playing a significant and essential role. He goes on in this passage to name how individuals within the church have particular callings: apostles, prophets, teachers, those who are given gifts of healing, forms of assistance, forms of leadership, various kinds of tongues (1 Cor. 12:28). Then he asks, "Are all apostles? Are all prophets? Are all teachers? Are all workers of miracle? Do all possess gifts of healing? Do all speak in tongues? Do all interpret?" (verses 29-30) And then he concludes, "But strive for the greater gifts. And I will show you a still more excellent way" (verse 31). What follows, to describe the more excellent way, is Paul's great hymn of love, which begins, "Though I speak with the tongues of mortals and of angels, but do not have love, I am a noisy gong or a clanging cymbal" (1 Cor. 13:1).

The poor and marginalized, the lonely and emotionally deprived, the abused and oppressed need to know who they are: persons loved by God, valued in their uniqueness, and called to live in the power of this love and convey it to others. Many of us who are not poor or marginalized, lonely or emotionally deprived, abused or oppressed, need to live in the power of this love and convey it to others. On Day Five of Week Two, we considered the sin of unbelief: refusing to accept the fact that God loves us. The total witness of scripture is focused at this point: God loves us with an unconditional, limitless love. Many people around us—the poor and marginalized, the lonely and emotionally deprived, the abused and oppressed—may not know this. It is our Christian opportunity to accept this love, claim it for ourselves, and share it with others.

REFLECTING AND RECORDING

Name someone, among people you know best, who you consider is a Mary.

Name someone you consider a Martha.

How does each of these individuals claim and reflect God's love? Does each feel loved by God?

✦ ✦ ✦

Name a person who you feel is struggling with self-identity, with knowing that he or she is loved by God.

Spend two or three minutes praying for this person.

❖   ❖   ❖

Are there groups of people in your community who need the Christian church to reach out to them in a deliberate way to share God's love?

❖   ❖   ❖

What can you do to inspire your church in such a ministry?

❖   ❖   ❖

DURING THE DAY

Pay close attention to all the people you meet today. Seek to say or do something that will affirm them as children of God.

DAY
5

The Mark of Christ's Indwelling

Beloved, since God loved us so much, we also ought to love one another. No one has ever seen God; if we love one another, God lives in us, and his love is perfected in us. By this we know that we abide in him and he in us, because he has given us of his Spirit. And we have seen and do testify that the Father has sent his Son as the Savior of the world. God abides in those who confess that Jesus is the Son of God, and they abide in God. So we have known and believe the love that God has for us. God is love, and those who abide in love abide in God, and God abides in them. Love has been perfected among us in this: that we may have boldness on the day of judgment, because as he is, so are we in this world. There is no fear in love, but perfect love casts out fear; for fear has to do with punishment, and whoever fears has not reached perfection in love. We love because he first loved us. Those who say, "I love God," and hate their brothers and sisters, are liars; for those who do not love a brother or sister whom they have seen, cannot love God whom they have not seen. The commandment we have from him is this: those who love God must love their brothers and sisters also.

—1 John 4:11-21

Julian of Norwich provides a marvelous definition of Christ's indwelling: "I saw that every kind of compassion which one has for one's fellow Christians in love is Christ in us" (*Showings*, 149). The contemporary writer Madeleine L'Engle, whom one day we will regard as we now regard Julian—as a saint with whom we need to keep company—teaches us why "compassion . . . exercised in love" is so essential in every age. Mark Trotter shares a telling incident from her life in a sermon.

[Madeleine L'Engle] and her husband live in the heart of New York City, Manhattan, where violence is a part of everyday life. They have a retreat in the Catskills, where they go on many weekends, and spend a great deal of time there in the summer.

They call it Crosswicks. It provides for them a world of peace, safety, away from the violence of their everyday life in New York. There they find a world of natural beauty, serenity, and peace—far removed from the ugliness and violence and breakouts of evil.

One Christmas their daughter gave them an icon—a picture of Mary and the baby Jesus. Madeleine loved it. She thought it was perfect for Crosswicks, so she took it there [when summer came] and nailed it to a tree by the stream where she would often go and meditate and pray.

The summer ended. They closed the cabin and returned to the city. The next spring, on their first visit to the cabin after a long winter, Madeleine went down to that special sanctuary by the stream. A terrible sight greeted her. Someone, at close range, had shot the icon—shattered it to pieces, and the pieces were lying on the ground. She picked up one of them and was shocked. It had the face of the baby Jesus on it and the bullet had gone straight into baby Jesus' head. It was obvious that whoever had done this had aimed the gun directly at Jesus.

Though Madeleine knows there are greater crimes than that vandalism, for her this was the very embodiment of what evil does. It invades our lives, destroying that which is precious to us. More often than not it is anonymous, silent, and invisible. It strikes out and makes us feel helpless and hopeless. We feel impotent to protect ourselves or protect those who are precious to us.

She said it took some time before she could return to that quiet spot where the icon had been destroyed. When she did return, she discovered something surprisingly wonderful. The tree that held the icon had absorbed the wound but continued to grow. You could hardly see where the icon had hung and where the gunshot had destroyed it. She wrote this:

"[I now find] my faith in the promise of Easter, of the resurrection. Not only of the Lord Jesus Christ but of us all; . . . not as a panacea . . . but as the reality which lights the day. [I believe that] God . . . will not create creatures able to ask questions only to be snuffed out before they can answer them. . . . The joyful God of love who shouted the galaxies into existence is not going to abandon any iota of his creation. So the icon tree for me is a symbol of God's concern, forever and always unto ages of ages, for all of us, every single one of us, no matter what we think or believe or deny" [from L'Engle, *The Irrational Season*].

God's concern for each one of us is activated and expressed by our concern for one another. There is the special need to express concern for those who have lost their way and are in sin. Julian reminds us that unless we look upon the sinner "with contrition with him, with compassion on him, and with holy desires to God for him," we will damage our own souls. The marvelous definition of Christ's indwelling quoted above is the conclusion of her observation:

> The soul which wants to be in rest should, when other men's sins come to mind, flee that as the pain of hell, seeking from God help against it. For the contemplation of other men's sins makes as it were a thick mist before the soul's eye, and during that time we cannot see the beauty of God, unless we can contemplate them with contrition with him, with compassion on him, and with holy desires to God for him. For without this it harasses and troubles and hinders the soul which contemplates them. . . .

> [H]e who is highest and closest to God may see himself sinful and needy along with me. And I who am the least and the lowest of those who will be saved may be comforted along with him who is highest.

> I saw that every kind of compassion which one has for one's fellow Christians in love is Christ in us. (*Showings*, 328, 333, 149)

REFLECTING AND RECORDING

Recall and record here an experience of your own similar to the one L'Engle described: Something happened that made you feel hopeless and helpless, impotent to protect something or someone precious, followed by an event or change that brought hope and life, confirming the fact and power of the Resurrection.

Spend a few minutes reflecting on Julian's claim that unless we look upon the sinner "with contrition with him, with compassion on him, and holy desires to God for him," we will damage our own souls.

Do you know someone living in sin for whom you need to show compassion? Can you readily name persons for whom you are expressing "holy desires to God"? These are searching questions, demanding our attention. Our response may indicate either a dreadful failure in our compassion or the mark of Christ in us as we express compassion.

Spend the balance of your time pondering Julian's confession: "I saw that every kind of compassion which one has for one's fellow Christians in love is Christ in us."

✤ ✤ ✤

DURING THE DAY

Make a telephone call, write a note, or personally visit someone for whom you need to show compassion.

DAY
6

The Greatest of These

If I speak in the tongues of mortals and of angels, but do not have love, I am a noisy gong or a clanging cymbal. And if I have prophetic powers, and understand all mysteries and all knowledge, and if I have all faith, so as to remove mountains, but do not have love, I am nothing. If I hand over my body so that I may boast, but do not have love, I gain nothing. Love is patient; love is kind; love is not envious or boastful or arrogant or rude. It does not insist on its own way; it is not irritable or resentful; it does not rejoice in wrongdoing, but rejoices in truth. It bears all things, believes all things, hopes all things, endures all things. Love never ends.

—1 Corinthians 13:1-8

Paul closed his great hymn of love, saying, "And now faith, hope, and love abide, these three; and the greatest of these is love" (1 Cor. 13:13). Visions, revelations, tongues of mortals and angels, miraculous manifestations, knowledge, prophecy—all are little compared to love. There is a sense in which there is nothing higher, in fact, nothing else in religion, but love. Spiritual writers say the heaven of heavens is love. John Wesley said,

> If you look for anything but more love, you are looking wide of the mark, you are getting out of the royal way.
>
> And when you are asking others, "Have you received this or that blessing?" if you mean anything but more love, you mean wrongly. You are leading them out of the way, and putting them upon a false scent.
>
> Settle it, then, in your heart that from the moment God has saved you from all sin, you are to aim at nothing more but more of that love described in the thirteenth chapter of Corinthians. You can go no higher than this until you are carried into Abraham's bosom. (*Joy of the Saints*, 327)

All are in need of love. During recess time at school a girl was seen playing by herself. That was always the case. No one played with her. The teacher kept a watchful eye on her and noticed that she went over to the corner of the school grounds, where there was a big tree. The girl reached up into the tree to a big branch, placed something there, and then ran away.

Naturally the teacher was suspicious. She thought the little girl might have stolen something and hidden it there. So later on she went to the tree, where she thought the little girl had placed the unknown item, and to her surprise, pulled out a piece of paper. On it was written a message, "Whoever finds this, I love you."

Everybody needs love. The whole Bible is a message left to us from God. It says, "Whoever finds this, I love you." *God loves each one of us as though each one of us were the only person in the world to love.* Over and over again, the scripture is clear—God is love. Spiritual writers like William Law sound this truth in different ways over and over again.

> **Wherever it comes, it comes as the blessing and happiness of every natural life, as the restorer of every lost perfection, a redeemer from all evil, a fulfiller of all righteousness, and a peace of God which passeth all understanding.** (*Spirit of Love*, 483)

> **Through all the universe of things nothing is uneasy, unsatisfied or restless but because it is not governed by love, or because its nature has not reached or attained the full birth of the spirit of love. For when that is done, every hunger is satisfied, and all complaining murmuring, accusing, resenting, revenging, and striving are as totally suppressed and overcome as the coldness, thickness, and horror of darkness are suppressed and overcome by the breaking forth of the light.** (*Spirit of Love*, 471)

> **If you ask why the spirit of love cannot be displeased, cannot be disappointed, cannot complain, accuse, resent, or murmur, it is because divine love desires nothing but itself, it is its own good, it has all when it has itself; . . . because nothing is good but itself and its own working; for love is God and he that dwelleth in God, dwelleth in love.** (*Spirit of Love*, 471)

REFLECTING AND RECORDING

Ponder prayerfully the following assertions made by William Law:

Love comes "as the restorer of every lost perfection."

✦ ✦ ✦

Love comes as "a redeemer from all evil."

✦ ✦ ✦

Love comes as "a fulfiller of all righteousness."

✦   ✦   ✦

Love comes as "a peace of God which passeth all understanding."

✦   ✦   ✦

Rewrite the second paragraph from William Law above in your own words.

If you are a part of a group sharing this workbook adventure, this is your fifth week of meeting. Does this experience suggest that an ongoing group in which you can share would support your spiritual growth? Begin to give this possibility some thought.

DURING THE DAY

If you were not able yesterday to make a telephone call, write a note, or personally visit someone for whom you need to show compassion, do so today. Find some times today to pray specifically for that person.

DAY
7

Being Holy Means Being Cordial

For though you might have ten thousand guardians in Christ, you do not have many fathers. Indeed, in Christ Jesus I became your father through the gospel. I appeal to you, then, be imitators of me. For this reason I sent you Timothy, who is my beloved and faithful child in the Lord, to remind you of my ways in Christ Jesus, as I teach them everywhere in every church.

—1 Corinthians 4:15-17

Be imitators of me, as I am of Christ.

—1 Corinthians 11:1

Teresa of Avila said, "The holier [people] are, the more sociable they should be." When I read that sentence, I thought of Antoine de Saint-Exupéry, the author of *The Little Prince*. As one of the first aviators, he flew in North Africa and South America at the beginning of the century. Out of that experience he wrote a beautiful book about flying, *Wind, Sand and Stars*. His plane had crashed in the North African desert, and surviving that ordeal changed his life. He came out of that experience with a heightened expectation of what life can be—of what human beings are capable of and what they can achieve, as well as what little time we have to reach the possibilities.

Early in *Wind, Sand and Stars*, he tells about his first flight, delivering mail. He and all the postal workers and government clerks were transported to the air depot just at daybreak. He describes the faces of people in the bus with him, most of them lifeless. Of one of them, he said,

> Old bureaucrat, my comrade, it is not you who are to blame. No one ever helped you to escape. You, like a termite, built your peace by blocking up with cement every chink and cranny through which the light might pierce. You rolled yourself up into a ball in your genteel security, in routine, in the stifling conventions of provincial life, raising a modest rampart against the winds and the tides and the stars. You have chosen not to be perturbed by great problems, having trouble enough to forget your own fate as man. You

are not the dweller upon an errant planet and do not ask yourself questions to which there are no answers. You are a petty bourgeois of Toulouse. Nobody grasped you by the shoulder while there was still time. Now the clay of which you were shaped has dried and hardened, and naught in you will ever awaken the sleeping musician, the poet, the astronomer that possibly inhabited you in the beginning. (Saint-Exupéry, *Wind, Sand and Stars*, 23)

Teresa knew how important it is to call people out, to listen nonjudgmentally, and to affirm. She connected that kind of relating to others with holiness. Her observation "The holier they are, the more sociable they should be" is in a list of advice Teresa gave to the sisters of her order.

Try, then, . . . to be as pleasant as you can, without offending God, and to get on as well as you can with those you have to deal with, so that they may like talking to you and want to follow your way of life and conversation, and not be frightened and put off by virtue. This is very important for nuns: the holier they are, the more sociable they should be with their sisters. Although you may be very sorry if all your sisters' conversation is not just as you would like it to be, never keep aloof from them if you wish to help them and have their love. . . . So try . . . to bear in mind that God does not pay great attention to all the trifling matters which occupy you, and do not allow these things to make your spirit quail and your courage fade, for if you do that you may lose many blessings. As I have said, let your intention be upright and your will determined not to offend God. But do not let your soul dwell in seclusion, or, instead of acquiring holiness, you will develop many imperfections, which the devil will implant in you in other ways, in which case . . . you will not do the good that you might, either to yourselves or to others. (*Complete Works of Saint Teresa*, II:181)

REFLECTING AND RECORDING

Can you think of an individual who turned you off to Christianity because of the way he or she talked about or lived the Christian faith or what the person demanded in respect to the Christian faith? Describe that person here.

Name the person who has most attracted you to the faith and made you want to be like him or her and describe that individual.

Teresa knew that we can easily get depressed by our failure to attract others with our Christian life and witness. So she counseled, "[D]o not let your soul dwell in seclusion, or, instead of acquiring holiness, you will develop many imperfections." Spend some time examining how you may be treating yourself when you fail and how you may be preventing your own growth.

Consider this truth expressed by Teresa. To punish ourselves, to keep putting ourselves down, does not contribute to our sanctity; rather, it reveals and underscores our imperfections.

DURING THE DAY

Seek to live in such a way that others "may like talking to you and want to follow your way of life and conversation."

Group Meeting
for Week Five

INTRODUCTION

On Day Three of Week Four we focused on living in "a continual state of prayer," or praying *without ceasing*. The disciplines required for such prayerful living are *intention* and *attention*. We must be purposeful if we are to follow through on our intentions and if we are really going to *attend* to what is going on around us. We can't be lazy.

This principle is particularly important in the group sharing process. It is easy to take the lazy route in our group participation. The temptation is to "play it safe" and not risk being honest and vulnerable.

Energy is another issue. Listening and speaking demand physical as well as emotional energy. So the temptation is to hold back, to be only half-present, not to invest the attention and focus essential for full participation.

I urge you to withstand these temptations. The sharing sessions are important. Don't underestimate the value of each member's contribution. Remain sensitive to the possibility of sinking into laziness.

SHARING TOGETHER

1. Begin your time together with prayer by the leader or someone else (consulted ahead of time). Then sing a chorus or a couple of stanzas of a hymn everyone knows.
2. You are drawing to the close of this workbook venture. You have only two more planned group meetings, so your group may want to discuss the future. Would the group like to stay together for a longer time? Are there resources (books, tapes, periodicals) that the group would like to use corporately? If you are all attending the same church, think about ways you might share the experience you have had with others.
3. Ask each participant to share the most challenging and meaningful insight or experience gained during this week.
4. Spend five or ten minutes discussing how persons in the group address God. What are favorite names or titles for God and why? What titles cause problems for people? Why?

5. Spend ten or twelve minutes discussing how love transforms relationships, circumstances, goals, directions, and values; share experiences of such transformation.

6. Take ten to fifteen minutes probing these questions: Which groups of people in our community need the Christian church to reach out in love? When people come to my church do they readily experience a loving community?

7. Invite one to two persons to share an experience when something made them feel hopeless and helpless, then hope and life returned, confirming the fact and power of the Resurrection (Reflecting and Recording, Day Five.)

8. Invite a couple of group members to read their version of Law's second paragraph from Day Six.

9. Ask a few individuals to tell the group about a person who attracted them to the faith and made them want to be like her or him.

10. Spend the balance of your time discussing Julian's claim that unless we look upon the sinner with contrition with that person, compassion on that person, and holy desires to God for that person, we will damage our own souls.

PRAYING TOGETHER

Teresa of Avila said, "God is well pleased to see a soul humbly taking His Son as Mediator, and yet loving Him so much that . . . it realizes its unworthiness" (*Complete Works of Saint Teresa*, I:141). And William Law said, "Praying is not speaking forth eloquently, but simply, the true desire of the heart" (*Spirit of Prayer*, Pryr-2.3-48). Remember this as you pray together now in a conversational style. This kind of spontaneous conversational prayer is a creative and guiding source in our corporate life. Close your time together by inviting as many as will to offer brief prayers growing out of tonight's sharing. Before you begin this, ask if anyone in the group has specific prayer requests, especially areas where he or she or others need guidance. When as many as wish to have prayed, close by inviting all to pray together the Lord's Prayer.

WEEK
Six

Shaping the
Inner Self

DAY
1

Coming Home to Oneself

We are distinctively marked as human beings by our inner struggle. Ever since the Fall, a foreign element has been present in our nature, making us rebellious and self-centered, desirous of being "as God." William Law says that in each of us there is an inward person of pride, the diabolical self. Paul, in his letter to the Galatians, gave full expression to this experience.

> *Here is my advice, Live your whole life in the Spirit and you will not satisfy the desires of your lower nature. For the whole energy of the lower nature is set against the Spirit, while the whole power of the Spirit is contrary to the lower nature. Here is the conflict, and that is why you are not able to do what you want to do. But if you follow the leading of the Spirit, you stand clear of the Law.*
>
> —Galatians 5:16-18, JBPHILLIPS

The great moment in the story of the prodigal son, who had demanded his inheritance early and forsaken home and family for life in a "far country," was when he "came to himself." He had engaged in uncontrolled revelry and succumbed to unchecked passions. His riotous living led to the pigpen. Full of shame and guilt, bereft of his fair-weather friends, lonely and homesick, he experienced a shock of recognition. Even the servants back home had it better than he. Jews were commanded not to eat pork. Here he was, a Jew, reduced to feeding the swine and eating what he fed to them. What a position of shame! An agonizing self-struggle with a world of meaning is gathered up in that one phrase "when he came to himself" (Luke 15:17).

The saints are always calling us to that shock of recognition—to see ourselves where we are, and as we are. William Law focuses on the "inward Strong Man of pride."

The inward Strong Man of pride, the diabolical Self, has his higher Works within; he dwells in the Strength of the Heart, and has every Power and Faculty of the Soul offering continual Incense to him.

His Memory, his Will, his Understanding, and Imagination, are always at work for him and for no one else. His Memory is the faithful Repository of all the fine Things that Self has ever done; and lest any Thing of them should be lost or forgotten, she is continually setting them before his Eyes. His Will, though it has all the World before it, yet goes after Nothing but as Self sends it. His Understanding is ever upon the Stretch for new Projects to enlarge the Dominions of Self; and if this fails, Imagination comes in as the last and truest Support of Self; she makes him a King and mighty Lord of Castles in the Air.

This is that full-born natural Self that must be pulled out of the Heart, and totally denied, or there can be no Disciple of Christ; which is only saying this plain Truth, that the apostate Self-idolatrous Nature of the old Man must be put off, or there can be no new Creature in Christ. (*Works*, IX:109–10)

Our unredeemed pride employs our capacities of *memory*, *will*, *understanding*, and *imagination* to keep us self-centered, away from a life yielded to Christ. Unredeemed pride is the heart of what Paul calls our "lower nature" which is in constant battle against the Spirit.

Even when we are not successful in our pride-directed life, our memory brings to mind all the things we have done *on our own*, so we resist any notion of surrender to Christ. Our will, ever so strong and controlling, is subject to our prideful self— our "lower nature," so we make choices without a Christ perspective. Our understanding, conditioned by our selfish desires, gives direction to our will for egotistic decisions that gratify "the flesh." Our imagination provides flights of fantasy that prevent us from facing reality and coming home to ourselves.

REFLECTING AND RECORDING

Reread paragraph two of the passage above by Law. Read it slowly for understanding.

✤ ✤ ✤

Law insists that *memory*, *will*, *understanding*, and *imagination* keep the strong person of pride in control of our lives. Look at your life, your spiritual journey, and see how the strong person of pride has used these faculties of memory, will, understanding, and imagination to prevent spiritual growth, surrender to Christ, vocational expression, and relationships that are Christ-centered rather than selfishly controlled. Make notes about how each faculty has functioned to prevent spiritual growth.

Memory

Will

Understanding

Imagination

Read again Law's third paragraph above. Reflect on the personal relevance of the radical suggestion that the "full-born natural Self . . . must be pulled out of the Heart and totally denied" if you are to be a disciple of Christ.

❖   ❖   ❖

DURING THE DAY

Printed on page 203 is the following stanza of a hymn by Charles Wesley. It is a prayer. Cut it out and either carry it with you or put it in a place where you will see it often. Make it your prayer many times daily.

> Come, Saviour, come and make me whole,
> Entirely all my sins remove;
> To perfect health restore my soul,
> To perfect holiness and love.

DAY
2

The Inner Self—
Generating Life or Death

Yesterday we considered "coming home to oneself," which requires a shock of recognition—to see ourselves *where* we are and *as* we are. The great moment in the prodigal son's life was when he *came to himself.* What happened afterward is really incidental to the crucial nature of that moment. Life is a "coming-home-to-oneself." It mattered that the father received the young man back into the family circle, that he expressed his love by bringing in friends to celebrate, that he symbolized the restored relationship by giving the robe and the ring. But suppose the father hadn't responded in such gracious love? Suppose he had acted with "nose out of joint" like the stubborn, self-righteous brother. It would have mattered to the returning son, of course, but I have an idea that reaction would not have thrown the young man. He had come home to *himself.* The personal resources engendered by his coming-home-ness would have allowed him to overcome such a rebuff. We get a hint of this new identity in his request: "Treat me like one of your hired hands" (Luke 15:19).

In our scripture lesson yesterday (Gal. 5:16-18), Paul describes the inner struggle that marks our humanity: "The whole energy of the lower nature is set against the Spirit, while the whole power of the Spirit is contrary to the lower nature" (verse 17, JBPHILLIPS). Paul gives dramatic detail to the rest of this struggle:

The activities of the lower nature are obvious. Here is a list: sexual immorality, impurity of mind, sensuality, worship of false gods, witchcraft, hatred, strife, jealousy, bad temper, rivalry, factions, party-spirit, envy, drunkenness, orgies and things like that. I solemnly assure you, as I did before, that those who indulge in such things will never inherit God's kingdom. The Spirit, however, produces in human life fruits such as these: love, joy, peace, patience, kindness, generosity, fidelity, tolerance and self-control—and no law exists against any of them. Those who belong to Christ Jesus have crucified their lower nature with all that it loved and lusted for.

—Galatians 5:19-24, JBPHILLIPS

In a passage we considered on Day Six of Week Four, William Law makes the case thus:

> Our desire is not only thus powerful and productive of real effects, but it is always alive, always working and creating in us. I say creating, for it has no less power, it perpetually generates either life or death in us. (*Christian Devotion*, 85)

The battleground is inside. We will be unable to choose which exterior battles are even worth fighting unless we seriously engage in the inner warfare. As Christians we are to respond to life and make our decisions out of the experience of God in Christ touching the core of our lives and freeing us from the bondage of sin. God's forgiveness and acceptance give self-worth and meaning, affirming us as persons and calling us to a life of holiness. In every situation we are to act out of that experience. Paul expresses this state of being by saying, "It is no longer I who live, but it is Christ who lives in me. And the life I now live in the flesh I live by faith in the Son of God, who loved me and gave himself for me" (Gal. 2:20).

Whatever else the indwelling of Christ means, and it means a "lifefull," it certainly calls us to act in relationship to persons and in moral decision making in the way God in Christ has acted in relation to us. Situational decisions are to be made not according to the whim of the moment nor by the rule of passion nor by the pressure of prevailing patterns nor by whether I can get away with it or not but according to who I am by the power of Christ. Recall William Law's comments, from Week Four, Day Six, on the efficacy of prayer as a kindling and creating power, forming and transforming the soul "into everything that its desires reach after." This thought can direct us as we engage in this ongoing struggle between the spirit of God within us and what Paul calls our "lower nature." Jacques Ellul describes the struggle:

> The Christian life is always an agony, that is, a final decisive conflict: thus it means that constant and actual presence in our hearts of the two elements of judgment and grace. But it is this very fact that ensures our liberty. We are free, because at every moment in our lives we are both judged and pardoned, and are consequently placed in a new situation, free from fatalism, and from the bondage to sinful habit.

Christ judges and forgives. As we claim that action in our lives, we are freed from the sins that burden us down, freed from meaningless guilt and the threat of death, thus set free to be the unique sons and daughters of God we were created to be.

Tomorrow we will talk more about this inner struggle, the dynamic of prayer in engaging that struggle, and our union and communion with God through the indwelling Christ. For now, let William Law speak to us again:

The book of all books is in your own heart, in which are written and engraven the deepest lessons of divine instruction; learn therefore to be deeply attentive to the presence of God in your hearts, who is always speaking, always instructing, always illuminating that heart that is attentive to him.

Here you will meet the divine light in its proper place, in that depth of your souls, where the birth of the Son of God and the proceeding of the Holy Ghost are always ready to spring up in you.

And be assured of this, that so much as you have of inward love and adherence to his holy light and spirit within you, so much as you have of real unaffected humility and meekness, so much as you are dead to your own will and self-love, so much as you have of purity of heart, so much, and no more, nor any further, do you see and know the truths of God. (*Joy of the Saints*, 90)

REFLECTING AND RECORDING

Spend a few minutes reflecting on Law's claim that "all outward power that we exercise in the things about us is but as a shadow in comparison of that inward power that resides in our will, imagination, and desires" (*Christian Devotion*, 85; see Week Four, Day Five).

How true is it that our *desire* "perpetually generates either life or death in us"? Recall and record briefly your desires generating either life or death.

Life

Death

DURING THE DAY

Continue using Charles Wesley's hymn stanza as your prayer.

DAY
3

Cleaning House

Spiritual writers often refer to our interior self as an "inner castle" or a palace. These metaphors call to mind one of Jesus' stories.

When the unclean spirit has gone out of a person, it wanders through waterless regions looking for a resting place, but not finding any, it says, "I will return to my house from which I came." When it comes, it finds it swept and put in order. Then it goes and brings seven other spirits more evil than itself, and they enter and live there; and the last state of that person is worse than the first.
—Luke 11:24-26

It's a poignant story. This unnamed person once harbored a demon. Jesus doesn't tell us whether the demon was "cast out" (exorcised), expelled, or simply left. It went wandering about the desert in search of lodging. Finding none, it returned to the original dwelling. In the meantime, the person had cleaned house—swept and scrubbed, and put the inner castle in order. Seeing this new condition, the demon recruited seven friends to join it in residence there.

Whatever you think about demons, it's clear Jesus took them seriously. A big part of his ministry was casting out demons. In this story, whatever was bothering the person was both a personal and a powerful reality. Unquestionably, the person must have experienced tremendous relief when the demon departed. Perhaps he or she could now sleep at night and felt better. The cloud of gloom constantly hovering overhead gave way to blue skies. Depression turned into confidence and hope. The person had a new lease on life; the house was clean.

Then it happened. Far worse than before, the old demon with seven companions moved in. The belief in that day was that demons couldn't simply run loose; they had to dwell somewhere. The big lesson: It is not enough simply to clean house, merely to drive out a demon; the now clean palace must be occupied. William Barclay says, "The empty soul is the soul in peril" (*The Gospel of Luke*, 152). My friend William Ritter preached a wonderful sermon based on this story.

Professionals in the diet business tell me that most of the people who take it off, put it right back on. Along with a little more. They are so disciplined, so careful, so focused—for a while. But having reached their goal, they return to old ways of eating. Pretty soon, they're back where they started. Or worse.

The same is true in the drug rehab business. Only the stakes are higher. Some years ago I received a personalized tour of a locked treatment facility for adolescents. It was a six-week residential program. At that time, it was considered to be the finest in the nation. I was impressed by the competence of the staff, the compassion of the caregivers and the creativity of the curriculum. But I was quickly sobered when the therapist said that over 50 percent of the people on first release will return.

So last night I called a friend of mine who works in the field of chemical addiction. He's as good as they come. And he's as up-to-date as they come. I asked him if the relapse rate has declined in recent years, given the improvement in treatment modalities. And I was saddened to learn that it hasn't. He said that things haven't changed in the last quarter century. It is still assumed that 30 percent of those released from a first hospitalization will relapse within 90 days, and an additional 30–35 percent will relapse in 180 days.

When you apply the relapse factor to imprisoned criminals, only the name changes. Among penal authorities, it is called *recidivism*. But the rate of return to jail certainly equals that of drug rehabilitation—and may even be higher.

We see the relapse factor in every sphere of life. Bad habits broken are bad habits slipped back into, just when you think you've conquered them for good. Destructive thoughts, against which you have barred the front door, reenter through unlocked windows in the basement of the soul. Crippling emotions defy even the best therapies and reappear in moments of weakness and vulnerability. Husbands and wives target harmful postures for removal, only to find that (twenty years later) they are still doing the same dumb stuff that has worked against them from the outset. In fact, most every marriage has one issue that simply won't go away . . . that threads itself through the history of the union . . . reappearing at regular intervals. It's hard to keep a clean house clean.

Teresa of Avila sees Jesus our Lord on the throne of our inner palace and urges us to consider how we might treat it differently, knowing who occupies this space.

And now let us imagine that we have within us a palace of priceless worth, built entirely of gold and precious stones—a palace, in short, fit for so great a Lord. Imagine that it is partly your doing that this palace should be what it is—and this is really true, for there is no building so beautiful as a soul that is pure and full of virtues, and, the greater these

virtues are, the more brilliantly do the stones shine. Imagine that within the palace dwells this great King, Who has vouchsafed to become your Father, and Who is seated upon a throne of supreme price—namely, your heart. . . .

I think, if I had understood then, as I do now, how this great King really dwells within this little palace of my soul, I should not have left Him alone so often, but should have stayed with Him and never have allowed His dwelling-place to get so dirty. . . .

And, as He refuses to force our will, He takes what we give Him but does not give Himself wholly until *He sees that* we are giving ourselves wholly to Him. (*Complete Works of Saint Teresa*, II:117–18)

REFLECTING AND RECORDING

We will give this issue more attention tomorrow. For now, examine the "relapse" factor in your life. Has there been a pattern of "cleaning house" and keeping it clean for a period of time, only to fall back into an old pattern? Briefly describe that pattern as you have experienced it in the past few years.

Reread Teresa's last paragraph. Do you feel that you do not have all of Christ you may desire because you have not yielded a part of your life entirely to him? Spend some time in serious self-examination.

✦   ✦   ✦

DURING THE DAY

Continue using Charles Wesley's hymn stanza as your prayer.

D A Y
4

Christ in Us—Our Only Salvation

I am the true vine, and my Father is the vinegrower. He removes every branch in me that bears no fruit. Every branch that bears fruit he prunes to make it bear more fruit. You have already been cleansed by the word that I have spoken to you. Abide in me as I abide in you. Just as the branch cannot bear fruit by itself unless it abides in the vine, neither can you unless you abide in me. I am the vine, you are the branches. Those who abide in me and I in them bear much fruit, because apart from me you can do nothing.

—John 15:1-5

Paul was captured by Jesus' offer, "abide in me as I abide in you," words Jesus spoke to his disciples. Paul was a person of one subject, as his writings reflect. To the Corinthians, he wrote, "I determined to know nothing among you, save Jesus Christ and him crucified." Under the guidance of the Holy Spirit, he coined the phrase "in Christ."

Blessed be the God and Father of our Lord Jesus Christ, who has blessed us in Christ with every spiritual blessing in the heavenly places, just as he chose us in Christ before the foundation of the world to be holy and blameless before him in love.

—Ephesians 1:3-4

Paul's experience on the Damascus Road had led him to the conviction that not only is Christ God's agent of change, he is absolutely central in the Father's strategy to bring us to full salvation. William Law makes a dramatic statement about this: "A Christ not in us, is the same thing as a Christ not ours." Law goes on to say:

If we are only so far with Christ, as to own and receive the history of his birth, person, and character, if this is all that we have of him, we are as much without him, as much left to ourselves, as little helped by him, as those evil spirits which cried out, "We know thee, who thou art, the holy one of God." (*Spirit of Prayer,* Pryr-1.1-43)

SHAPING THE INNER SELF 161

It is the language of Scripture that Christ in us is our hope of glory, that Christ formed in us, growing and raising his own life and spirit in us, is our only salvation. . . . For since the serpent, sin, death and hell are all essentially within us, the very growth of our nature, must not our redemption be equally inward, an inward essential death to this state of our souls, and an inward growth of a contrary life within us? (*Spirit of Prayer*, Pryr-1.1-44)

Yesterday we considered the fact that cleaning house is not enough. We must order our lives around the fact that Jesus is Lord; he occupies the throne of our inner castle. Being Christian means far more than avoiding the bad. We cannot build our Christian "house" on negatives. Our morality must be more than what we don't do. Jesus was very clear: *we must bear fruit.* His most fiery display of anger was not when he drove the moneychangers from the temple but when he cursed the barren fig tree.

Our "relapse factor" is connected with our failure to recognize and cultivate awareness of the indwelling Christ. Freed from some addiction, having defeated some harmful and shameful habit, it is easy to grow smug. We get comfortable and even cocky, forgetting that what once tripped us up can trip us up again. So we must abide in Christ. Paul makes an amazing claim in Romans 6:5-6:

For if we have been united with him in a death like his, we will certainly be united with him in a resurrection like his. We know that our old self was crucified with him so that the body of sin might be destroyed, and we might no longer be enslaved to sin.

In his writings Paul stresses the uniqueness of Christ's sacrifice for sin. There was, in fact, no one else qualified to die for the sins of the world, whether by holiness, obedience, or status. In addition, Jesus not only died *for* sin but also died *to* sin. He moved beyond the power of sin. But the power of Christ didn't stop there. Paul asserts that by our union with Jesus in his death, we also have died to sin. "For we know that our old self was crucified with him so that the body of sin might be destroyed, and we might no longer be enslaved to sin. For whoever has died is freed from sin" (Rom. 6:6-7). Paul reiterates a few verses later, "Sin will have no dominion over you" (Rom. 6:14).

William Law connects this entire understanding of the power of Christ to free us from sin to our life of spiritual discipline and how we pray.

The spiritual life is nothing else but the working of the spirit of God within us, and therefore our own silence must be a great part of our preparation for it, and much speaking or delight in it will be often no small hindrance of that good which we can only have from hearing what the spirit and voice of God speaks within us.

This is not enough known by religious persons; they rejoice in kindling a fire of their own, and delight too much in hearing of their own voice and so lose that inward unction from above which can alone newly create their hearts.

To speak with the tongues of men or angels on religious matters is a much less thing than to know how to stay the mind upon God, and abide with him in the closet of our hearts, observing, loving, adoring and obeying his holy power within us.

I have written very largely on the spiritual life, and he understands not my writings, nor the end of them, who does not see that their whole drift is to call all Christians to a God and Christ within them as the only possible life, light and power of all goodness they can ever have. I invite all people to the marriage of the Lamb, but no one to myself. (*Joy of the Saints*, 364)

REFLECTING AND RECORDING

Spend some time pondering Law's statement "A Christ not in us, is the same as a Christ not ours." You may want to reread the first passage by Law quoted above.

✠   ✠   ✠

Law says that our own silence must be a great part of our preparation for the spirit of God to work within us. He says that too many of us delight in hearing our own voice so we "lose that inward unction from above which can alone newly create" our hearts.

Try to remember some occasions when silence played a big role in your spiritual growth, allowed you to hear God or find divine guidance. Record that experience here.

Does your ability or inability to identify a meaningful experience of silence suggest a need for more silence in your life? Spend some time thinking about how you will practice silence as a spiritual discipline.

✠   ✠   ✠

Law uses what may be a new, even strange, expression for you: "that inward unction from above." Having read the above material for today, what does that mean to you? Write two or three sentences.

DURING THE DAY

Try to find a thirty-minute time period today when you can be completely silent in a place away from noise as much as possible.

DAY
5

The Manifestation of Jesus Christ in Our Inward New Person

Centralia, Pennsylvania, is a mining town, or it was when coal was king. More than thirty years ago, a fire broke out in the maze of tunnels and shafts that honeycomb the earth beneath the town. State and even federal mine authorities joined local forces to extinguish the fire, but these combined forces were never completely successful. The fire still burns somewhere in those tunnels. Now and then a puff of smoke will break through the surface to let everyone know the fire is lurking somewhere in that labyrinth of tunnels and shafts in the bowels of the ground.

This is a powerful reminder of the fact of our lives that we have been considering the last four days. All the saints with whom I have sought to keep company believed that our only hope of preventing the smoldering possibility of relapse into sin is to yield ourselves completely to Christ and allow him to manifest his life and spirit in our inward new person. William Law states the case eloquently:

All our salvation consists in the manifestation of the nature, life and spirit of Jesus Christ in our inward new man. This alone is Christian redemption, this alone redeems, renews and regains the first life of God in the soul of man. Everything besides this is self, is fiction, is propriety, is own will. . . .

Enter therefore with all your heart into this truth, let your eye be always upon it, do everything in view of it, try everything by the truth of it, love nothing but for the sake of it. Wherever you go, whatever you do, at home or abroad, in the field or at church, do all in a desire of union with Christ, in imitation of his tempers and inclinations, and look upon all as nothing but that which exercises and increases the spirit and life of Christ in your soul. (*Joy of the Saints*, 172)

"Do all in a desire of union with Christ." This means that the presence of Christ is not to be sought and/or experienced only on occasion. We must develop daily disciplines that keep us aware of Christ within. Our devotional reading, our meditation and prayer especially should be focused on *recognizing and cultivating awareness of the indwelling Christ.* Julian of Norwich says:

> Beseeching is a true and grace-giving, lasting will of the soul, which is oned [made one] and fastened to the will of our Lord, by the sweet and secret working of the Holy Ghost. (*Revelations of Divine Love*, 114)

This focus in our spiritual disciplines gives direction and strength for the imitation of Christ's "tempers and inclinations"; thus we model and manifest the presence of Christ in the world. Someone has defined a saint as "one in whom Christ is felt to live again."

REFLECTING AND RECORDING

Accepting the definition, according to Jacophone da Todi, that a saint is "one in whom Christ is felt to live again," name the person of your acquaintance who would come closest to being a saint.

_____

What characteristics of that individual cause you to think of him or her as a saint? What are this person's characteristic attitudes and actions? Write some sentences describing this person.

Law urges us to "do all in a desire of union with Christ, in imitation of his tempers and inclinations." Ponder this advice for a few minutes, then record here the *tempers* and *inclinations* of Jesus that you need most to cultivate.

Spend a few minutes reflecting on Law's advice to "look upon all as nothing but that which exercises and increases the spirit and life of Christ in your soul."

✦ ✦ ✦

What are two or three things in your life that you must count as nothing, habits that you must give up, attitudes that you must surrender in order for the spirit and life of Christ to increase in your soul? Make some notes.

Now, to the right of the first paragraph of the passage by Law above, write his message in your own words.

✦ ✦ ✦

DURING THE DAY

Seek to be aware throughout the day of the things you do, the encounters you have, your responses to situations that either diminish or increase the "spirit and life of Christ in your soul." Also find another thirty-minute period of silence. During that time, seek to fasten your soul on God and make it one with the divine will.

DAY
6

I Am the Reason Jesus Came to Earth

In his book *What's So Amazing about Grace?* Philip Yancey wrote that he found in Mozart's *Requiem* a prayer that he now uses daily: "Remember, merciful Jesu, that I am the cause of your journey." On Day Three of Week One, we focused on this dynamic coming from another direction. Julian of Norwich made the fantastic claim that "it is God's will that I see myself as much bound to him in love, as if all that he hath done he had done for me [alone]." We live boldly and in full awareness of grace when we remind ourselves of this truth in our praying. Likewise we should remind Jesus of why he came. It is not presumptuous to pray thus. We don't get to heaven by *being* and *doing* good. It's all grace. We cry Help! and God responds. Yesterday we quoted Julian of Norwich on prayer:

> Beseeching is a true and grace-giving, lasting will of the soul, which is oned and fastened to the will of our Lord, by the sweet and secret working of the Holy Ghost.

She continues her teaching with this grace-filled affirmation:

> I am the ground of thy beseeching. First, it is my will that thou have it—and seeing that I make thee to desire it, and seeing that I make thee to beseech it and thou beseechest it, how could it then be that shouldst not have thy beseeching? . . .
>
> For all the things that our good Lord himself maketh us to beseech, these he hath ordained to us from without-beginning. . . .
>
> And when we come into our bliss, it shall be given us as a part of our joy, with his endless worshipful thanks. (*Revelations of Divine Love*, 113–14)

Brother Lawrence, like many others, entered a monastic order believing that he was giving up this world's happiness to become a monk. He discovered a much deeper happiness than he had ever imagined. Brother Lawrence, reflecting on this turn of events, said to God, "You have outwitted me." Isn't that a delightful phrase? And what a testimony to the providence of God.

SHAPING THE INNER SELF 167

It is this providence Julian talks about in terms of prayer. To be in relationship with God demands prayer. Yet as God invites and inspires us to pray, God has already ordained that we should have that for which we pray. That's grace and providence dynamically at work within us. The word *providence* comes from the same root as our word *provide*. God's providence is flavored by God's grace. The Christian view of reality asserts there is a power greater than our powers. This God will provide and care for us often in surprising ways, which makes us echo Brother Lawrence, "You have outwitted me," O God.

I came to be the president of Asbury Theological Seminary convinced that God was calling me. But I came kicking and screaming. It was not what I wanted to do. I was blissfully happy and my life was filled with meaning as a pastor. I didn't want to give up preaching to the same people every Sunday, being present as pastor in the deepest, most significant times of people's lives: births, baptisms, marriages, deaths. Besides, the church was growing. Our outreach ministry and mission in Memphis and around the world was expanding and increasing in effectiveness. I had a unique TV/radio ministry called "Perceptions"—a sixty-second message responding to persons' felt needs, providing encouragement, hope, and challenge. Because of "Perceptions," I was known throughout the city and enjoyed the positive response of people far beyond my congregation. Hardly a day would pass without a specific affirming response to this special ministry. Not only did I not want to leave "my" congregation, I didn't want to leave "my" city where my twelve years as a pastor had been rich and rewarding. The cumulative influence of those years had given me a great platform for ministry and impact.

Along with that ministry, which was growing daily, and a congregation that challenged me, fed my soul, and gave meaning and indescribable joy, two of my adult children were living in Memphis. I didn't want to leave them. For six months I struggled with the invitation of the seminary trustees to be their president. They were clear that they were being led by God. Why could I not discern this as God's call? They were so sure.

I struggled. If this was God's call, God was asking too much. Finally it came clear. How that clarity came is another story. It is enough to say I felt the job to be God's will, and I was not pleased at all. I responded reluctantly, even grudgingly. I yielded, but without excitement, anticipation, or joy. My attitude was, "This is what I *have* to do."

God, "you have outwitted me." The richness of my life in a community of prayer, hearing many times weekly the witness of men and women who are passionately in love with Jesus and desirous of pleasing him, participating in a kingdom enterprise that is sending persons to the ends of the world to proclaim the gospel and spread scriptural holiness—I could not have imagined such joy and meaning as I have had during my tenure at Asbury. And I thought I was giving up something, sacrificing.

This popular epigram expresses the strange movement of God in our lives:

> I asked for riches that I might be happy.
> I was given poverty that I might be wise.
>
> I asked for power that I might have the praise of all.
> I was given weakness that I might feel the need of God.
>
> I asked for all things that I might enjoy life.
> I was given life that I might enjoy all things.
>
> Almost despite myself my unspoken prayers were answered.

REFLECTING AND RECORDING

Recall and record briefly an experience when you thought that you had messed things up, but they came out better than you planned.

Recall and record a time and experience when you thought you had lost everything but realized you had found something that you never imagined.

Spend the balance of your time allowing these words of Julian's to sink into your soul—relish the *grace* they express: "When we come into our bliss, it shall be given us as a part of our joy, with his endless worshipful thanks."

⟡ ⟡ ⟡

DURING THE DAY

Continue seeking to be aware throughout the day of the things you do, the encounters you have, your responses to situations that either diminish or increase the "spirit and life of Christ in your soul."

DAY
7

Acting Our Way into Christlikeness

*When he came to Nazareth, where he had been brought up, Jesus went to the syna-
gogue on the sabbath day, as was his custom. He stood up to read, and the scroll of the
prophet Isaiah was given to him. He unrolled the scroll and found the place where it
was written:*

> *"The Spirit of the Lord is upon me,*
> *because he has anointed me*
> *to bring good news to the poor.*
> *He has sent me to proclaim release to the captives*
> *and recovery of sight to the blind,*
> *to let the oppressed go free,*
> *to proclaim the year of the Lord's favor."*

*And he rolled up the scroll, gave it back to the attendant, and sat down. The eyes
of all in the synagogue were fixed on him. Then he began to say to them, "Today
this scripture has been fulfilled in your hearing."*

—Luke 4:16–21

Being Christian is a means of grace. Simply seeking to be like Christ, constantly
asking "What would Jesus do?" shapes us into his likeness. John Wesley taught a
lot about means of grace. He listed five means of grace: prayer, scripture, holy communion, fasting, and Christian conferencing. These he labeled *acts of piety*. Then
there were what he called *prudential* means of grace, or acts of mercy. He described
them simply as "doing no harm" and "doing all the good you can."

On Days Three and Four of this week, we considered the fact that it is not
enough to clean house. Unless we cultivate an awareness of the indwelling Christ,
allow him to occupy the throne of our "interior castle," seven demons may replace
the one we have cast out. We connected the "relapse factor" (falling back into old
patterns, habits, and addictions) with our failure to recognize and cultivate awareness
of the indwelling Christ. We must make this awareness concrete in our actions.

I have never seen a person who prayed his or her way into Christlikeness. Nor have I seen individuals who worshiped or studied their way into Christlikeness, but I have seen countless people who acted their way into Christlikeness. Oh, they were praying people, and they were disciplined in regular corporate worship, and they studied—immersing themselves in scripture. But they became Christlike through deliberately, self-consciously, intentionally seeking "to be like Christ." Brother Lawrence said:

> That we ought, once for all, heartily to put our whole trust in God, and make a full surrender of ourselves to Him, secure that he would not deceive us . . . . We ought not to be weary of doing little things for the love of God, who regards not the greatness of the work, but the love with which it is performed . . . . We should not wonder if, in the beginning, we often failed in our endeavors, but that at last we should gain a habit, which will naturally produce its acts in us, without our care, and to our exceeding great delight . . . . The whole substance of religion was faith, hope and love, by the practice of which we become united to the will of God; . . . that all besides is indifferent, and to be used only as a means that we may arrive at our end, and be swallowed up therein, by faith and love. (*Conversations and Letters*, 16–17)

For about three years now, I have had a letter in my Bible. It is from a dear friend named Pauline Hord. One paragraph of that letter says, "Maxie, teach your students to study thoroughly Luke 4:18, and when their time of ministry comes, call them to remember that there are hundreds of thousands in prisons who need to hear the message of the Savior."

Let me tell you about Pauline. She is now over ninety years old. For many years she has had a double passion: to teach people to read and write and to minister to people in prison. As a young woman, she was inspired by Dr. Frank Laubach, apostle for the illiterate, to teach people how to read and write.

At age eighty-eight, she was still involved in her literacy work—teaching a hundred and fifty schoolteachers in the public school system of Memphis a new system of literacy. Along the way, she combined her commitment to literacy with her passion for prison ministry. When I arrived in Memphis in 1982, Pauline was driving one hundred miles in one direction to Parchman prison in Mississippi to teach prisoners to read and write and to witness to them about Jesus. After about eight years, her eyesight failed, and we recruited someone to drive her to Parchman each Wednesday to spend the day.

Some of you may remember a program called "Points of Light," in which President George Bush sought to recognize people who were doing outstanding work in cities across America—bringing light in different kinds of ways. I nominated Pauline Hord for that award; she was elected as one of the "Points of Light" in

Memphis and subsequently was nominated to receive a national award. On an occasion when President Bush was coming to Memphis, he decided to meet with the eight persons in Memphis who had been nominated for this award. When Pauline was invited to meet with President Bush on the Wednesday when he would arrive, Pauline apologized, saying Wednesday was her day to work at Parchman. She was not willing to give up that ministry to prisoners in order to meet with the President.

I had a layover at the airport in Memphis one day after I had left to become the president of Asbury Seminary. It was about 6:30 in the evening, and I called Pauline on the phone. I could tell she was tired; I heard the weariness in her voice. She told me she had just come from spending the day in a new prison about forty miles from Memphis, teaching thirty volunteers a new literacy method, in order that they could teach those prisoners to read and write. About a week after that conversation I received the letter that means so much to me. Pauline apologized for her weariness and wanted to encourage me in my ministry. So she challenged me to teach our students to study thoroughly Luke 4:18. You know what that passage is? It is Jesus' affirmation of his ministry in the synagogue of Nazareth. He read from the scroll of the prophet Isaiah,

> *The Spirit of the Lord is upon me,*
> *because he has anointed me*
> *to bring good news to the poor.*
> *He has sent me to proclaim release to the captives*
> *and recovery of sight to the blind,*
> *to let the oppressed go free,*
> *to proclaim the year of the Lord's favor.*

Pauline is one of the most Christlike persons I know. She is a prayer warrior. She never misses worship on Sunday unless she is ill. She was part of many study groups within the life of our church—in fact has led a number of them. All of that was important to her, but really, *she acted her way into Christlikeness.*

REFLECTING AND RECORDING

Name someone you know who acted his or her way into Christlikeness.

Describe that person in a couple of paragraphs. What makes him or her like Christ? How does he act, relate, share? How would you characterize her attitudes? his or her inclinations and tempers?

Go back to Day Five of this week. In your reflecting and recording you were asked to record the tempers and inclinations of Jesus that you need most to cultivate. Look at your recordings that day. If you cultivated these tempers and inclinations, would you be acting your way into Christlikeness? What else might you add?

✠   ✠   ✠

During the Day

Continue seeking to be aware throughout the day of the things you do, the encounters you have, your responses to situations that either diminish or increase the "spirit and life of Christ in your soul."

Group Meeting
for Week Six

Introduction

NOTE: For this session the leader should provide a chalkboard. (See 7, 8, and 9 of Sharing Together.)

Last week you may have discussed whether your group wants to continue meeting. If so, here are two possibilities to consider.

1. Select two or three weeks from this workbook that were especially difficult or meaningful. Repeat those weeks in more depth as an extension of your time together.

2. Decide that you are going to continue your group, using another resource. You may appoint two or three members to bring resource suggestions to the

group next week. If this workbook style is meaningful, there are several others in the series:

- *The Workbook of Living Prayer*
- *The Workbook of Intercessory Prayer*
- *The Workbook on Spiritual Disciplines*
- *The Workbook on Becoming Alive in Christ*
- *The Workbook on Coping as Christians*
- *The Workbook on the Christian Walk*
- *The Workbook on Christians Under Construction and in Recovery*
- *The Workbook on Loving the Jesus Way*
- *The Workbook on the Seven Deadly Sins*
- *The Workbook on Virtues and the Fruit of the Spirit*

Another possibility is for one or two persons to decide they will recruit and lead a group through this workbook. Many people are looking for a small-group experience, and this is a way to respond to their need.

SHARING TOGETHER

1. On Day One, we focused on unredeemed pride, which uses our capacities of memory, will, understanding, and imagination to keep us self-centered, away from a life yielded to Christ. Spend ten or twelve minutes discussing this dynamic, sharing how these faculties have prevented spiritual growth.

2. Invite at least one participant to share a personal experience (or the experience of someone else, preserving anonymity) in which desires "perpetually generate *death*" (Reflecting and Recording, Day Two).

3. Now invite people to share experiences in which desires generate life.

4. Invite someone to read paragraphs two and three of the passage from Teresa on Day Three. Then let the group members spend ten to twelve minutes discussing whether they believe this is true and the implications for their spiritual growth.

5. According to William Law (Day Four), our silence must be a great part of our preparation for the spirit of God to work within us. Invite someone to share an experience when silence played a role in spiritual growth, hearing God, or finding divine guidance.

6. Spend five to ten minutes discussing Law's claim: "A Christ not in us, is the same as a Christ not ours."

7. Invite the group to turn to Reflecting and Recording on Day Five. Let everyone review the primary characteristics of the person he or she named as coming closest to being a saint. Using chalkboard or newsprint, the leader will write down the characteristics called out by members of the group. Let

each member name only one characteristic at a time. List as many characteristics as possible from the group.

8. Consider the list and underline characteristics common to everyone's description. Talk briefly about how to cultivate these characteristics.

9. Law urges us to "do all in our desire of union with Christ, in imitation of his tempers and inclinations" (Day Five). Ask each member to name one or two tempers or inclinations of Jesus he or she needs most to cultivate. The leader will write them on the board as they are named.

10. Now spend just a few minutes talking about what this exercise reveals about our common growth needs.

11. Invite a person to share an experience when she thought she had messed things up, but they came out better than she planned (Day Six).

12. Invite a person to share an experience when he thought he had lost everything but realized he had found something he never imagined.

13. Spend what time you have left discussing the discipline of acting our way into Christlikeness.

PRAYING TOGETHER

As you begin your prayer time, turn to Day One, During the Day. Sing this hymn stanza by Charles Wesley through twice to the tune of "Amazing Grace."

1. Invite the group to share prayer concerns—self, family, church, community. As these are shared, the leader will write them on the board.

2. Now invite the group to enter a time of prayer with some person praying for each of the concerns listed.

3. Close with the Lord's Prayer.

WEEK
Seven

The
Commitment
We Make

DAY
1

The Natural State of Our Tempers

On Day One of Week One, we considered this claim of William Law's:

> It is the state of our will that makes the state of our life; when we receive anything from God and do everything for God, everything does us the same good and helps us to the same degree of happiness.
>
> Sickness and health, prosperity and adversity, bless and purify such a soul in the same degree; as it turns everything towards God, so everything becomes divine to it. For he that seeks God in everything is sure to find God in everything. (*Christian Devotion*, 51)

I have some friends who have dramatically proven this is so. Mat and Cindy Lipscomb came to our church as single young adults early in my ministry at Christ Church, Memphis. They were outstanding young professionals, both highly successful. They became a vibrant part of our singles ministry. I watched their beginning courtship and shared and counseled with them as their love deepened and they married.

The babies came—three beautiful girls, Rainey, Lacey, Jesse Anne—and I shared in their baptisms. They became personal and family friends. Mat and Cindy were devoted parents, putting Christ first in their family, faithfully immersing their children in the church and in Christian teaching.

About two weeks before Easter, 1999, Cindy took the three girls on a train trip to Chicago. Their grandmother, Cindy's mother, accompanied them. It was to be a special "girls' thing." And it was—until the return train trip back to Memphis. In the middle of the night, the train collided with an eighteen-wheel tractor-trailer truck loaded with long steel beams.

The two older Lipscomb girls, Rainey and Lacey, were spending the night with one of their mother's best friends who, along with her daughter and granddaughter, had accompanied them on the trip. They were in a sleeping car near the front of the train and were still up, looking out the window. Cindy and her youngest daughter, Jesse Anne, with Cindy's mother, were in a sleeper car to the rear of the train and had just settled down for the night. The two older Lipscomb girls, Cindy's friend June, and June's granddaughter were killed instantly. The other child in that group lost part of her leg.

Who can imagine the pain? the devastating anguish? the sense of helplessness, hopelessness, and loss? the tormenting questions that must have raged in Cindy and Mat's minds? Why? Why this tragic waste? The heartbreak—they were absolutely crushed. Yet, I have never experienced a more radiant, convincing witness to the empowering presence of Christ.

When asked how they would live with the awful pain and loss, Mat and Cindy had a ready answer: "I can do all things through Christ who gives me strength." That word comes from Paul's testimony to the Philippians:

> *I rejoice in the Lord greatly that now at last you have revived your concern for me; indeed, you were concerned for me, but had no opportunity to show it. Not that I am referring to being in need; for I have learned to be content with whatever I have. I know what it is to have little, and I know what it is to have plenty. In any and all circumstances I have learned the secret of being well-fed and of going hungry, of having plenty and of being in need. I can do all things through him who strengthens me.*
>
> –Philippians 4:10-13

Mat and Cindy lived through their ordeal out of what William Law calls "the natural state of our tempers." He makes the case that we cannot forever keep hidden "our inward state."

> **The natural state of our tempers has a variety of covers under which they lie concealed at times, both from ourselves and others; but when this or that accident happens to displace such or such a cover, then that which lay hidden under it breaks forth. And then we vainly think that this or that outward occasion has not shown us how we are within, but has only infused or put into us a wrath, or grief, or envy which is not our natural state, or of our own growth, or has all that it has from our own inward state.**
>
> **But this is mere blindness and self-deceit, for it is as impossible for the mind to have any grief or wrath or joy, but what it has all from its own inward state, as for the instrument to give forth any other harmony or discord but that which is within and from itself.**
>
> **Persons, things and occurrences may strike our instrument improperly and variously, but as we are in ourselves, such is our outward sound, whatever strikes us. If our inward state is the renewed life of Christ within us, then every thing and occasion, let it be what it will, only makes the same life to sound forth and show itself.** (*Spirit of Love,* 409–10)

In the immediate aftermath of the accident, television and newspaper reporters pressed Mat and Cindy for "stories"—responses to the unbelievable and terrible tragedy. At first, they evaded the reporters, but then they began to have second thoughts. Maybe they should talk. Mat called me from Chicago to discuss what might be their right response to the media. I never will forget his statement: "We want to be good stewards of this tragedy." Wow! I could do no less than encourage him to talk to the media, but on his own terms. He and Cindy did, and they continue to make a powerful witness. In every TV and newspaper interview they found a way to affirm Christ's abiding presence and strength and to express forgiveness for the man who caused the accident.

Mat and Cindy proved Law right. "If our inward state is the renewed life of Christ within us, then every thing and occasion, let it be what it will, only makes the same life to sound forth and show itself."

REFLECTING AND RECORDING

Spend a few minutes reflecting on Law's assertion: "It is as impossible for the mind to have any grief or wrath or joy, but what it has all from its own inward state."

Now reflect on this: "Persons, things and occurrences may strike our instrument improperly and variously, but as we are in ourselves, such is our outward sound, whatever strikes us." Rewrite this statement in your own words.

Name three individuals you know who have experienced tragedy, painful circumstances, personal loss, or broken relationships.

1.

2.

3.

Examine what you know about these persons' responses, how they are doing today, and how their experiences have shaped their lives. How did their responses differ? What was the determining factor in how they handled and were shaped by their circumstances?

✤   ✤   ✤

Examine your own life. What is the natural state of your temper? Do you have adequate resources to be a good steward of tragedy that may come?

✤   ✤   ✤

DURING THE DAY

Call or write one of the people you listed above, expressing appreciation for his or her witness in the face of an ordeal.

D A Y
2

My Grace Is Sufficient

On behalf of such a one I will boast, but on my own behalf I will not boast, except of my weaknesses. But if I wish to boast, I will not be a fool, for I will be speaking the truth. But I refrain from it, so that no one may think better of me than what is seen in me or heard from me, even considering the exceptional character of the revelations. Therefore, to keep me from being too elated, a thorn was given me in the flesh, a messenger of Satan to torment me, to keep me from being too elated. Three times I appealed to the Lord about this, that it would leave me, but he said to me, "My grace is sufficient for you, for power is made perfect in weakness." So, I will boast all the more gladly of my weaknesses, so that the power of Christ may dwell in me. Therefore I am content with weaknesses, insults, hardships, persecutions, and calamities for the sake of Christ; for whenever I am weak, then I am strong.

—2 Corinthians 12:5-10

Karl Barth, the eminent theologian, once preached a sermon entitled "Six Words Are Enough." His scripture text was, "My grace is sufficient for you" (2 Cor. 12:9). He said it was the briefest text he had ever preached on and added, "The wonderful spice of it lies in its brevity." Then he gave this powerful testimony:

> Some of you may have heard that in the last forty years I have written many books, some large. I will freely and frankly and gladly admit that these six words say much more and much better things than all the heaps of paper with which I have surrounded myself. They are enough—which cannot be said even remotely of my books. What may be good in my books can be at most that from afar they point to what these six words say. And when my books are long since outdated and forgotten, and every book in the world with them, these words will still shine with everlasting fullness: "My grace is sufficient for you." (in *Classics Devotional Bible*, 1367)

Christians through the ages have found it so. Brother Lawrence witnessed to it at the mundane level of everyday life. He said:

> **That we ought to act with God in the greatest simplicity, speaking to Him frankly and plainly, and imploring His assistance in our affairs just as they happen. That God never failed to grant it, as he had often experienced.**
>
> **That he had been lately sent into Burgundy to buy the provision of wine for the Society, which was a very unwelcome task to him, because he had no turn for business, and because he was lame and could not go about the boat but by rolling himself over the casks. That, however, he gave himself no uneasiness about it, nor about the purchase of the wine. That he said to God it *was His business he was about*, and that afterwards he found it very well performed. That, he had been sent to Auvergne the year before upon the same account; that he could not tell how the matter passed, but that it proved very well.**
>
> **So, likewise, in his business in the kitchen (to which he had naturally a great aversion), having accustomed himself to do everything there for the love of God, and with prayer, upon all occasions, for His grace to do his work well, he had found everything easy during the fifteen years he had been employed there.** (*Conversations and Letters*, 9)

Yesterday we considered the dramatic witness of Mat and Cindy Lipscomb who found God's grace—the presence and power of Christ—sufficient for the experience of devastating loss. We need to know that God is sufficient for every problem, every difficulty, every broken heart, and every human sorrow. But we also need to know with Brother Lawrence that God is sufficient for the demands and pressures of everyday living:

- for boring days that drag on week in and week out because we are stuck in an unchallenging job that requires only rote performance,
- for our job as a parent that is so daily and so seemingly unrewarding,
- for a Christian discipleship that calls for obedience but has yet to reward us with any sign that we have made a difference,

God's grace is sufficient for:

- the single mother who is left to bear the total burden of child-rearing because a selfish husband-father has forsaken his responsibility,
- a faithful minister who has spent years serving in small congregations in out-of-the-way places,
- missionaries who don't have dramatic stories to tell of conversions and healings but keep returning to their "fields" because deep down they know that's where God wants them,
- schoolteachers and nurses and others who are never in the limelight but who give all their energy every day.

Brother Lawrence found the secret of the sufficiency of God's grace in our everyday living—*do everything for the love of God and with prayer.*

REFLECTING AND RECORDING

In the space above, list persons and/or situations you think about for which God's grace is sufficient.

In what area of your everyday living do you need to experience the sufficiency of God's grace? Make some notes.

Paul heard the Lord say, "My grace is sufficient for you, for power is made perfect in weakness." Recall an experience that was true for you: the Lord's strength was made perfect in your weakness, his grace was sufficient. Describe that experience here.

Memorize this verse: "My grace is sufficient for you, for power is made perfect in weakness."

During the Day

Deliberately seek to recall and quote this verse aloud or to yourself throughout the day.

DAY
3

A Continual Walk with God

Let's continue our consideration of Brother Lawrence's counsel: Do everything for the love of God and with prayer. He wrote:

> I have received today two books and a letter from Sister ———, who is preparing to make her "profession," and upon that account desires the prayers of your holy Community, and yours in particular . . . I will send

you one of these books which treat of the *Presence of God*, a subject which, in my opinion, contains the whole spiritual life; and it seems to me that whoever duly practices it will soon become spiritual.

I know that for the right practice of it the heart must be empty of all else, because God wills to possess the heart alone; and as He cannot possess it alone unless it be empty of all besides, so he cannot work in it what He would unless it be left vacant to Him.

There is not in the world a kind of life more sweet and delightful than that of a continual walk with God.

Those only can comprehend it who practice and experience it; yet I do not advise you to do it from that motive.

It is not pleasure which we ought to seek in this exercise; but let us do it from the motive of love, and because God would have us so walk. (*Conversations and Letters*, 26)

"God wills to possess the heart alone." This echoes Jesus' teaching when he quotes the prophet Isaiah:

The Lord said:
Because these people draw near with their mouths
*   and honor me with their lips,*
*   while their hearts are far from me,*
and their worship of me is a human commandment learned by rote . . .
—Isaiah 29:13

On Day Three of Week Six, we learned that many spiritual writers considered the heart as our inner palace where Jesus must sit on the throne. In this sense, the "heart must be empty of all else, because God wills to possess the heart *alone*." Many of these writers also looked at the heart, as did scripture, as the seat of the will, where decisions of loyalty and passion were made. These two notions are merged in the testimony of an inmate, Weimar Quijano, in Bellavista Prison, Medellin, Colombia. My friend Jeanine Brabon ministers there. Built to house 1,500 inmates, but now packed with over 5,000, it has been one of the worst prisons in that country. Its culture was the culture of death—50 people slaughtered every month, human heads kicked about like soccer balls on the recreation ground, homosexual rapes. But God has done a mighty work and dramatic transformations have taken place. David Miller's book *The Lord of Bellavista* tells the dramatic story of a prison transformed. Near the close of the book, he gives a poignant summary of the change that has taken place.

People will remember Juan Carlos Londoño for many reasons, perhaps the most remarkable being that his murder was the only violent death recorded inside Bellavista Jail in 1996. The same prison that once claimed 50 lives a month has averaged only one homicide per year since 1990, when Oscar Osorio envisioned God wrapping the jail in his hand and received divine orders to raise white flags and pray. During the same six-year period, Oscar baptized 514 inmates in a makeshift baptistery in the prison chapel. Christian conversions have replaced murders as Bellavista's most impressive statistic.

Colombia's law enforcement community is aware of the change inside the jail. Many find it difficult to believe that an evangelical awakening could pacify the most violent prison in the Western world. Dr. Orlando Lopez, Bellavista's vice-governor, who directs Industrial and Educational Services in the jail, does not. Lopez has observed the change firsthand.

"Truthfully, the Lord has his hand on Bellavista," Lopez told a visiting journalist one day in the prison cafeteria. "The violence here has diminished 90 per cent. This is due to the careful job the prison personnel are doing and to prayer. We have prayer groups in every cell block."

"People are beginning to comprehend that praying in a cell block is effective. Inmates form a different outlook on life. The religious factor has rehabilitated people. That's where you see the importance of the gospel inside Bellavista Jail. In spite of the fact that this is the most crowded jail in the country, men are changing the way they live."(142)

Weimar is one of those who has been transformed. His heart, the seat of his will, is controlled by Jesus. Jesus sits on throne of the inner palace of his soul. From the Bellavista prison he wrote to Jeanine Brabon:

> My first Christmas here, I wept and wept. I had absolutely no hope. Then I found Jesus as my Savior. Now Christmas is holy delight because the King has found room in my heart. I cannot contain the joy of what Jesus is to me. What an opportunity I have here in prison! I have a twenty-seven–year sentence, yet I am totally free to celebrate Christmas. The greatest way I know is telling others about Jesus! "Born to die that man might live, came to earth new life to give."

For Jesus to occupy the throne of our lives, we must yield our will to him. This is not a one-time yielding but a daily surrender. And why should we make that surrender? Because no one cares for us as does Jesus. He has purchased our salvation and provided us freedom by his death on the cross. While "there is not in the world a kind of life more sweet and delightful than that of a continual walk with God," we walk with God, not for pleasure, but from the "motive of love."

REFLECTING AND RECORDING

The following is a time line from age 5 to 95 in 10-year increments. Designate with an X the point when you made a conscious decision to accept Christ, exercising your own will and making willful decisions.

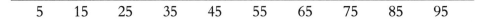

    5   15   25   35   45   55   65   75   85   95

Take a sweeping look at your life and designate with check marks (✓) above the time line periods or points when you were most yielded to Christ. Below the line mark with zeroes (0) the times when you were least yielded, maybe even rebellious. Register occasions of deliberate or internal response and commitment at higher points than your "normal" Christian walk. Occasions when you knew you were consciously resisting God's will would be at a point below the line. Seek to plot your continual walk with God.

✛   ✛   ✛

Write a brief prayer expressing yourself to God in relation to your past walk and your commitment about the future.

DURING THE DAY

Try to share with at least one person today what your experience has been as you reflect on your continual walk with God. You may want to invite that person to examine his or her life in a similar way.

DAY
4

Humility In Balance

In a sermon entitled "Table Manners," my friend Bill Ritter, minister in Birmingham, Michigan, quoted a powerful first-person story.

> During my second month of nursing school, our professor gave us a pop quiz. I was a conscientious student and had breezed through the questions, until I read the last one: "What is the first name of the woman who cleans the school?"
>
> Surely this was some kind of joke. I had seen the cleaning woman several times. She was tall, dark-haired and in her fifties. But how would I know her name? I handed in my paper, leaving the answer blank. Then I heard another student ask if the last question would count toward our grade. "Absolutely," said the professor. "In your careers you will meet many people. All are significant. Each deserves your attention and care, even if all you do is smile and say hello."
>
> I've never forgotten that lesson. I've also learned that her name is Dorothy.

This story reminded me of William Law's challenge: "Let it [humility] be as a garment wherewith you are . . . girt." He encompassed that admonition with this fuller word:

> Nothing is in vain, or without profit, to the humble soul; like the bee, it takes its honey ever from bitter herbs; it stands always in a state of divine growth; and everything that falls upon it, is like a dew of heaven to it. Shut up yourself therefore in this form of humility, all good is enclosed in it; it is a water of heaven, that turns the fire of the fallen soul, into the meekness of the divine life. . . . Let it be as a garment wherewith you are always covered, and the girdle with which you are girt; breathe nothing [but in and from its spirit; see nothing but with its eyes; hear nothing] but with its ears; and then, whether you are in the

church or out of the church; hearing the praises of God, or receiving wrongs from . . . the world, all will be edification, and every thing will help forward your growth in the life of God. (*Spirit of Prayer*, Pryr-2.3-28)

To be humble is to see yourself as one with others, to think yourself no better or no less than another. It is to value another enough to pay attention to her or him and to regard that individual as a person of infinite worth. Jesus is our model. One of the most beautiful descriptions of him is Philippians 2:5-11:

Let the same mind be in you that was in Christ Jesus, who, though he was in the form of God, did not regard equality with God as something to be exploited, but emptied himself, taking the form of a slave, being born in human likeness. And being found in human form, he humbled himself and became obedient to the point of death—even death on a cross. Therefore God also highly exalted him and gave him the name that is above every name, so that at the name of Jesus every knee should bend, in heaven and on earth and under the earth, and every tongue should confess that Jesus Christ is Lord, to the glory of God the Father.

This is not only a description of Jesus; it is a call to us. Preceding this passage, Paul says, "Let each of you look not to your own interests, but to the interests of others" (verse 4). Then he challenges us: "Let this mind be in you which was also in Christ Jesus." That's a tall order. Read again the scriptural description of Jesus.

He humbled himself and became obedient, emptied himself, did not grasp the equality of God that was his. Can we wear that garment of humility? William Law uses a marvelous image: "like the bee it [humility] takes its honey ever from bitter herbs." Isn't that what Jesus did? The bitter herb of the cross was transformed. God exalted the humbled Jesus and gave him a name above every name. Yet even before he had reached that point of ultimate humility—obedience unto death, Jesus had clothed himself in that garment. He taught with authority:

When you are invited by someone to a wedding banquet, do not sit down at the place of honor, in case someone more distinguished than you has been invited by your host; and the host who invited both of you may come and say to you, "Give this person your place," and then in disgrace you would start to take the lowest place. But when you are invited, go and sit down at the lowest place, so that when your host comes, he may say to you, "Friend, move up higher"; then you will be honored in the presence of all who sit at the table with you. For all who exalt themselves will be humbled, and those who humble themselves will be exalted.

—Luke 14:8-11

The writers with whom we are keeping company wrote much about humility. It was absolutely essential in their view. Yet, they saw how easy it was to distort humility. Julian of Norwich provided this perspective:

[Christ says], Do not accuse yourself that your tribulation and your woe is all your fault; for I do not want you to be immoderately depressed or sorrowful. (*Showings*, 331)

Thus it is our enemy who wants to retard us with his false suggestions of fear about our wretchedness because of the pain which he threatens us with. For it is his purpose to make us so depressed and so sad in this matter that we should forget the blessed contemplation of our everlasting friend. (*Showings*, 329)

It is a most lovely humility in a sinful soul, made by the mercy and grace of the Holy Spirit, when we are willing and glad to accept the scourging and the chastising which our Lord himself wishes to give us. And it will be very tender and very easy, if we will only keep ourselves content with him and with all his works . . . We ought meekly and patiently to bear and suffer the penance which God himself gives us, with recollection of his blessed Passion. For when we recall his blessed Passion, with pity and love, then we suffer with him as his friends did who saw it. (*Showings*, 330)

We must keep our humility in balance. We are not to think more highly of ourselves than we ought to think, nor are we to fall into self-loathing and self-deprecation.

REFLECTING AND RECORDING

Spend a few minutes in self-examination. Are you prone to act from selfish ambition or conceit, thus needing constantly to pay attention to the needs of others? Or, are you too self-critical, blaming yourself too much, never thinking you are humble enough?

✦ ✦ ✦

Read again the introductory story for this day.

✦ ✦ ✦

Does the story remind you of people in your daily life whose names you don't even know? people to whom you need to pay attention?

✦ ✦ ✦

Spend a few minutes reflecting on the following words from William Law: "Nothing is in vain, or without profit, to the humble soul; . . . everything that falls upon it, is like a dew of heaven."

DURING THE DAY

Move through this day seeing "nothing but with its [humility's] eyes," hearing "nothing but with its ears."

DAY
5

He Defrays All the Costs

America witnessed a Christian martyr in 1999. The television scenes are still vivid in my mind. On April 20, 1999, Columbine High School in Littleton, Colorado, became a killing field. Two students, armed with guns, bombs, and other explosives loosed their rage. TV cameras showed hundreds of students fleeing the buildings with their hands above their heads, so that the police squads who had been called in would not mistake them for the attackers. Thirteen people were killed and numerous others wounded. The two student killers committed suicide.

Many stories of courage and heroic action during those events have been told. The most dramatic and inspiring is that of Cassie Bernall. She had become a Christian only two years before and was a member of prayer group at school and a vibrant witness to her faith. Though it appeared early on that the student killers' rage was aimed at "jocks," those involved in competitive athletics, it seems that religion may have been an equal target. According to students, the killers screamed about God. One of them confronted Cassie, leveled a shotgun in her face, and asked if she believed in God. She paused only a moment, knowing the threat, and responded, "Yes, I do believe in God." And that was it. Her physical life was blasted away.

Cassie died faithful to God and witnessing to her faith. Her simple affirmation of faith, uttered in the last moments of her life, has turned this seventeen-year-old victim of the Columbine High School massacre into a modern-day martyr. Her faith and witness are penetrating and challenging the conscience of millions.

We don't know much about martyrdom firsthand. The chance that any of us will be called to be a martyr like Cassie is so remote, we doubtless have given it little thought. A word out of the Celtic tradition challenges us:

> Now there are three kinds of martyrdom which are counted as a cross to man, that is to say, white martyrdom, and green martyrdom, and red martyrdom.
>
> This is the white martyrdom to man, when he separates for the sake of God from everything he loves, although he suffer fasting or labour thereat.
>
> This is the green martyrdom to him, when by means of them (fasting and penance) he separates from his desires, or suffers toil in penance and repentance.
>
> This is the red martyrdom to him, endurance of a cross or destruction for Christ's sake, as has happened to the apostles in the persecution of the wicked and in teaching the law of God.
>
> These three kinds of martyrdom are comprised in the carnal ones who resort to good repentance, who separate from their desires, who pour forth their blood in fasting and in labour for Christ's sake. (*Joy of the Saints*, 234)

Over against that call is a great promise: Christ "defrays all the costs." Teresa of Avila connected the extravagant self-giving of Christ with prayer.

> **We must begin prayer by feeling no doubt that unless we allow ourselves to be defeated we are sure to succeed. This is certain, for however insignificant our conquest may be we shall come off with great gains.**
>
> **Never fear that the Lord Who invites us to drink of the fountain will allow us to die of thirst.** (*Living Water*, 27)

Was Teresa thinking of Isaiah's word?

> *Ho, everyone who thirsts,*
> *come to the waters;*
> *and you who have no money,*
> *come, buy and eat!*
> *Come, buy wine and milk*
> *without money and without price.*
> *Why do you spend your money for that which is not bread,*
> *and your labor for what does not satisfy?*
> *Listen carefully to me, and eat what is good,*
> *and delight yourselves in rich food.*
> *Incline your ear, and come to me.*
> —Isaiah 55:1-3

Teresa continues:

I have said it before and I shall often repeat it, for people who have not learnt our Lord's goodness by experience, but only know of it by faith, are often discouraged.

It is a great grace to have proved for oneself the friendship and caresses He bestows on those who walk by this way or prayer, and how, as it were, He defrays all the costs.

It does not surprise me that those who have never practised it should want the security of receiving some interest. You know that we receive a hundredfold even in this life, and that our Lord said, "Ask and you shall receive." If you do not believe Him it would be of little use for me to wear myself out with telling you. (*Living Water*, 27)

REFLECTING AND RECORDING

Consider the three kinds of martyrdom described in the passage from Celtic tradition. In the space below each "martyrdom," record your commitment. Of what do you need to repent? From what desires do you need to separate? Are you willing to "die" to these desires? Do you need to fast? Are you called to particular labors?

Separation from things loved

Separation from our desires

Fasting and labor for Christ's sake

Spend a few minutes reflecting on Teresa's claim that we must be willing to be defeated if we are to succeed in our life of prayer.

⊕   ⊕   ⊕

What does Teresa mean when she says our Lord "defrays all the costs" as it relates to grace and his friendship with us?

✣   ✣   ✣

DURING THE DAY

On page 203 you will find printed Teresa's word: "Never fear that the Lord Who invites us to drink of the fountain will allow us to die of thirst." Cut out this word and put it in a place where you will see it often. In the days ahead, keep claiming the promise.

D A Y
6

Forgiveness Is Essential

For if you forgive others their trespasses, your heavenly Father will also forgive you; but if you do not forgive others, neither will your Father forgive your trespasses.

—Matthew 6:14-15

Whenever you stand praying, forgive, if you have anything against anyone; so that your Father in heaven may also forgive you your trespasses.

—Mark 11:25-26

Teresa of Avila made a radical claim about how willingly we forgive when we have "approached so near to Mercy Himself."

I cannot believe that one who has approached so near to Mercy Himself, Who has shown the soul what it really is and all that God has pardoned it, would not instantly and most willingly forgive, and be at peace, and remain well-affected towards anyone who has injured her.

For the divine kindness and mercy shown her prove the immense love felt for her by the Almighty, and she is overjoyed at having an opportunity of showing love in return. (*Living Water*, 45)

My friends Mat and Cindy Lipscomb, whose story we read on Day One of this week, proved this power of forgiveness. The week after their daughters Rainey and Lacey were killed in the tragic train accident, they were interviewed on "The Today Show," a national TV program viewed by millions of people. The host on that show talked to them about the driver of the truck who had made the terrible mistake of trying to get across the track when the train was coming. He was being investigated regarding his responsibility for the accident, which took the lives of eleven people. The host asked Matt and Cindy what they thought about the truck driver. What were their feelings about the man who was responsible for the loss of their two daughters? I will never forget their response. Together they said something like this: "We can't imagine how bad that truck driver must be feeling. He made a terrible mistake—and all of us make mistakes. But certainly he would not do anything such as this willfully. Wherever he is, and we hope he is hearing this, we want him to know that we forgive him, and we pray for him."

Mat and Cindy had "approached," even received, "Mercy Himself." They knew firsthand God's forgiving and saving grace. They can understand better than most Teresa's additional word about forgiveness:

> **I repeat that I know a number of people whom our Lord has raised to supernatural things, giving them the prayer of contemplation I described, and though they have other faults and imperfections, I never saw one who was unforgiving, nor do I think it possible if these favours were from God.**
>
> **God always enriches the souls He visits. This is certain, for although the favour and consolation may pass away quickly, it is detected later on by the benefits it has left in the soul.** (*Living Water*, 45)

Recently I was having lunch with someone I had never met. A preacher friend had referred me to him, describing him as a person very involved in the life of the church and someone who would be interested in what our seminary is seeking to do. It was a remarkable time of sharing. It happens sometimes—an openness that defies our normal way of thinking—soul touching soul. Over the course of an hour-and-a-half lunch we shared deeply.

The man shared a moving story of a recent experience he and his wife had had during an Academy for Spiritual Formation, a growth and training ministry of Upper Room Ministries. The couple was participating in a reunion gathering of people who had completed the Academy program. The closing celebration was a foot-washing service. My new friend was seated next to the only African-American person in the group.

As the man got to this point in the story, tears began to course down his face. He had to stop occasionally because his voice would break. He apologized, indicating that as an attorney and a public speaker, this was not his normal style, but he was not embarrassed. He would smile and the tears would come as he continued to tell the story. He said that as he washed the black feet of his friend, a personal experience he had had only a few months before flooded his mind.

The man had visited his hometown in rural north Florida, where his father and his uncle were prominent citizens. Thinking back on his wonderful childhood, he said to his uncle, "Uncle John, we don't talk much about the past. You and Daddy are getting older, and I feel I need to know more about our roots—our history, our family background. Tell me about it."

The uncle paused for a minute, then said, "When you ask a question like that, Bill, you don't know what is going to come, do you?" He knew Bill's Christian commitment and his earnest effort to be a follower of Jesus. Perhaps he knew something about Bill's involvement with interracial institutions; or, maybe he knew none of this, but he continued, "Your grandfather's funeral was the last Ku Klux Klan funeral ever held in this county."

By this time my new friend's face was wet with tears and he was smiling. Referring back to the foot-washing service, he said, "I washed those black feet with a picture of my grandfather, a member of the Ku Klux Klan [in my mind] and thought of the reconciliation that had taken place that would lead to this. I knew that my life from now on had to be an expression of forgiving love."

REFLECTING AND RECORDING

Spend a few minutes pondering Teresa's word: "I cannot believe that one who has approached so near to Mercy Himself . . . would not instantly and most willingly forgive."

❖ ❖ ❖

What is your most memorable experience of being forgiven? Describe that experience.

Spend whatever time you have left reflecting on Jesus' word: "If you do not forgive . . . neither will your Father forgive your trespasses" (Matt. 6:14–15).

❖ ❖ ❖

DURING THE DAY

If there is someone you need to forgive, do so today, and let that person know you forgive.

If there is someone from whom you need to ask forgiveness, do so today.

Continue to claim Teresa's promise, which you were given yesterday.

DAY
7

Discipline Is Essential

I beseech you therefore, brethren, by the mercies of God, that you present your bodies a living sacrifice, holy, acceptable to God, which is your reasonable service. And do not be conformed to this world, but be transformed by the renewing of your mind, that you may prove what is that good and acceptable and perfect will of God.

—Romans 12:1-2, NKJV

T*he Living Bible* paraphrases the second verse of this passage, "Don't copy the behavior and customs of this world, but be a new and different person with a fresh newness in all you do and think." The witness of scripture and the spiritual writers of the ages is that to be a Christian is to change, to become a new person. When Paul says "that you may prove what is that good and acceptable and perfect will of God," he is saying that we are to model before the world what a Christ-abiding, Christ-filled life looks like. He makes his plea in a lot of different ways:

For this is the will of God, your sanctification.

—1 Thessalonians 4:3

You yourself are a guide to the blind, a light to those who are in darkness, an instructor of the foolish, a teacher of babes, having the form of knowledge and truth in the law. You, therefore, who teach another, do you not teach yourself? You who preach that [one] should not steal, do you steal? You who say, "Do not commit adultery," do you commit adultery? You who abhor idols, do you rob temples? You who make your boast in the law, do you dishonor God through breaking the law?

—Romans 2:19-23, NKJV

Ministers being ordained in the United Methodist tradition are asked a series of questions dating back to the days when John Wesley started the Methodist movement in the mid–eighteenth century. One of those questions is an almost overwhelming challenge: "Do you expect to be made perfect in this life?" There is only one answer: "By the grace of God." But then comes the follow-up question: "Are you earnestly striving after it [perfection]?" These questions are not unrealistic or radical in terms of the New Testament. One weakness of modern Christians is our reluctance to believe we can be completely transformed. As Christians, we are called to be demonstration plots of holiness, set down in a less-than-holy world.

In his marvelous book on understanding how God changes lives, *The Spirit of the Disciplines*, Dallas Willard lists two characteristics required if Christianity is going to guide our lives.

> First, it must take the need for human transformation as seriously as do modern revolutionary movements. The modern negative critique of Christianity arose in the first place because the church was not faithful to its own message—it failed to take human transformation seriously as a real, practical issue to be dealt with in realistic terms.
>
> Second, it needs to clarify and exemplify realistic methods of human transformation. It must show how the ordinary individuals who make up the human race today can become, through the grace of Christ, a love-filled, effective and powerful community. (ix)

We have confused the whole issue of works-righteousness. Because our Protestant understanding of justification by grace through faith contends that we cannot be saved by works, we fail to see the important role of disciplines in the order of salvation. The primary point of confusion is our connection of works with merit. We don't want to fall back into that trap—that our works in any way merit acceptance or salvation. But we need to recover the connection between grace and "works," if we want to call them that. The better designation is "disciplines." While they have no merit to our salvation, they are absolutely essential for "working out our salvation." Brother Lawrence contended that

> all bodily mortifications and other exercises are useless except as they serve to arrive at the union with God by love; . . . he had well considered this, and found it the shortest way to go straight to Him by a continual exercise of love and doing all things for His sake. . . .
>
> All possible kinds of mortification, if they were void of the love of God, could not efface a single sin. . . . We ought, without anxiety, to expect the pardon of our sins from the blood of Jesus Christ, only endeavoring to love Him with all our hearts. . . . God seemed to have granted the greatest favors to the greatest sinners, as more signal monuments of His mercy. (*Practice of the Presence*, 15)

[Brother Lawrence] thought neither of death nor of his sins, nor heaven nor hell, but of doing little things—being incapable of big ones—for the love of God. He had no need to trouble himself further, for whatever followed would be pleasing to God. (*Joy of the Saints*, 62)

Dallas Willard challenges us to live as Christians in today's world:

Holiness and devotion must now come forth from the closet and the chapel, to possess the street and the factory, the school room, and boardroom, the scientific laboratory and the governmental office. Instead of a select few making religion their life, with the power and inspiration realized through the spiritual disciplines, all of us can make our daily lives and vocations be "the house of God and the gate of heaven." It can—and must—happen. And it will happen. The living Christ will make it happen through us as we dwell with him in life appropriately disciplined in the spiritual Kingdom of God.

The Spirit of the Disciplines is nothing but the love of Jesus. (*Spirit of the Disciplines*, xii)

REFLECTING AND RECORDING

Read again the two characteristics Dallas Willard identifies as requirements if Christianity is going to be the guide to life which it alone can be. Spend a few minutes reflecting on his assessment.

✦ ✦ ✦

In your own experience, have you considered religious practices—disciplines— essential for your salvation?

✦ ✦ ✦

Have you hesitated to commit to disciplines because you did not want to substitute your "works" for God's grace in Jesus, which alone saves?

✦ ✦ ✦

Have you been guilty of connecting "works" (disciplines) with merit?

✦ ✦ ✦

Write a prayer expressing your response to *Keeping Company with the Saints* during these seven weeks.

DURING THE DAY
AND ALL THE DAYS FOLLOWING

Find ways to keep company with the saints—through the writings of those gone on to glory, but also in sharing with those "living saints" in your community.

Group Meeting
for Week Seven

INTRODUCTION

This is the last meeting designed for this group. You have talked about the possibility of continuing to meet. Conclude those plans. Whatever you choose to do, determine the time line, so that participants can make a clear commitment. Assign some persons to follow through with decisions that are made.

SHARING TOGETHER

Your sharing during this session will reflect on the entire seven-week experience. Leader, be sure to save enough time for responses to number 10.

1. Spend fifteen to eighteen minutes telling stories of persons you know who have experienced tragedy, painful circumstances, loss, or broken relationships. Reflect on the different responses to these experiences.
2. Have someone read the last paragraph by William Law on Day One.
3. Spend five to eight minutes talking about what it means to be a "good steward of tragedy."

4. Invite one or two participants to share an experience when the Lord's strength was made perfect in their weakness (Day Two).

5. Spend five to eight minutes discussing the need to keep humility in balance—not to think more highly of ourselves than we ought to think nor to fall into self-loathing and self-deprecation. Which is the more common violation for most persons in the group?

6. Invite two or three to share the martyrdom to which they most need to give themselves (Day Five): (a) Separation from things loved, (b) separation from desires, or (c) fasting and labor for Christ's sake. Be as specific as possible.

7. Spend eight to ten minutes discussing the two claims made by Teresa: (a) Our Lord "defrays all the costs"; (b) "Never fear that the Lord Who invites us to drink of the fountain will allow us to die of thirst."

8. Invite two or three persons to describe their most memorable experience of being forgiven.

9. Spend eight to ten minutes discussing the two statements by Dallas Willard on Day Seven. Is he right? What is the role of individuals in responding? the role of the church? How and to what degree are you and your current church responding to these requirements?

10. Spend the balance of your time sharing what these seven weeks have meant to individuals in the group—new insights, challenges, things they will have to work on.

PRAYING TOGETHER

Saint Teresa said of prayer:

> In prayer it is well to occupy ourselves sometimes in making acts of praise and love to God; in desires and resolutions to please Him in all things; in rejoicing at His goodness and that He is what He is; in desiring His honor and glory; in recommending ourselves to His mercy; also in simply placing ourselves before Him, beholding His greatness and His mercy, and, at the same time, our own vileness and misery, and then to let Him give us what He pleases, whether it be showers or aridity; for He knows better than we what is most suitable for us. (*Year with the Saints*, 266)

1. Spend two or three minutes in silence thinking and praying for individuals about whom you are concerned and to whom you may need to speak.

2. Invite each group member to share a commitment he or she has made or prayer requests. As each person shares, have a time of prayer—silent or oral, preferably oral—so that each person will be prayed for specifically.

3. Now ask two or three people to offer general prayers of thanksgiving for the eight-week experience and petitions for further growth and guidance.

4. A benediction is a blessing or greeting shared with another or by a group in parting. A variation on the traditional "passing of the peace" can serve as a benediction. Take a person's hand, look into his or her eyes, and say, "The peace of God be with you." That person responds, "And may God's peace be yours." Then that person takes the hand of the person next to him or her says, "The peace of God be with you," and receives the response, "And may God's peace be yours." Standing in a circle, let the leader "pass the peace," and let it go around the circle.

5. After the passing of the peace, speak to one another in a more spontaneous way. Move about to different individuals, saying whatever you feel is appropriate for your parting blessing to each individual. Or you may simply embrace the person and say nothing. In your own unique way, "bless" each group member who has shared this journey with you.

Bibliography

Barclay, William. "The Letter to the Hebrews," *The Daily Study Bible*. Edinburgh: The Saint Andrew Press, 1957.

Barclay, William. *The Gospel of Luke*. Philadelphia: The Westminster Press, 1953.

Barnhouse, Donald Grey. *Romans*. Grand Rapids, Mich.: Eerdmans, 1959.

Barth, Karl. "Six Words Are Enough," in *Classics Devotional Bible*. Grand Rapids, Mich.: Zondervan, 1996.

Brother Lawrence, *Brother Lawrence: His Conversations and Letters on the Practice of the Presence of God*. Cincinnati: The Forward Movement, 1941.

Brother Lawrence. *The Practice of the Presence of God*. Arranged and edited by Douglas V. Steere. Nashville, Tennessee: The Upper Room, 1950.

de Caussade, Jean-Pierre. *The Flame of Divine Love*. Edited by Robert Llewelyn. London: Darton, Longman and Todd Ltd., 1984.

Davis, Ron Lee, with James D. Denney. *Mistreated*. Portland, Oregon: Multnomah, 1989.

Fosdick, Harry Emerson. *The Meaning of Prayer*. New York: Association Press, 1916.

Julian of Norwich. *Daily Readings with Julian of Norwich*, vol. 1. Springfield, Ill.: Templegate Publishers, 1980.

Julian of Norwich. *Encounter with God's Love: Selected Writings of Julian of Norwich*. Selected, edited, and introduced by Keith Beasley-Topliffe. Nashville, Tenn.: Upper Room Books, 1998.

Julian of Norwich. *Julian of Norwich: Showings*. Translated and with an introduction by Edmund Colledge and James Walsh. New York: Paulist Press, 1978.

Julian of Norwich. *The Revelations of Divine Love of Julian of Norwich*. Translated by James Walsh. New York: Harper & Brothers, 1961.

Kepler, Thomas. *A Journey with the Saints*. Cleveland: The World Publishing Company, 1951.

Knight, George A. F. *Psalms, The Daily Study Bible Series*, Vol. I. Philadelphia: The Westminster Press, 1982.

Law, William. *A Serious Call to a Devout and Holy Life; The Spirit of Love*. Edited by Paul G. Stanwood. New York: Paulist Press, 1978.

Law, William. *The Life of Christian Devotion: Devotional Selections from the Works of William Law*. Edited by Mary Cooper Robb. Nashville: Abingdon Press, 1961.

Law, William. *The Pocket William Law*. Edited by Arthur W. Hopkinson. London: Latimer House Limited, 1950.

Law, William. *The Spirit of Prayer or The Soul Rising Out of the Vanity of Time, into the Riches of Eternity*, from the Christian Classics Ethereal Library at www.ccel.org/l/law/prayer/ Spirit_of_Prayer.txt.

Law, William. *The Works of the Reverend William Law, A.M.*, Vol. IX. London: Printed for J. Richardson, 1762.

Llewelyn, Robert. *The Joy of the Saints: Spiritual Readings throughout the Year*. Springfield, Ill.: Templegate Publishers, 1989.

McGinley, Phyllis. *Saint-Watching*. New York: The Viking Press, 1969.

Miller, David. *The Lord of Bellavista*. London: Triangle (SPCK), 1998.

Read, Harry. Saturday, 3 April in *Words of Life: The Bible Day by Day with the Salvation Army*, January–April 1999. London: Hodder & Stoughton, 1999.

Saint-Exupéry, Antoine de. *Wind, Sand and Stars*, New York: Harcourt, Brace and Company, Inc., 1940.

Spurgeon, Charles H. *All of Grace*. Grand Rapids, Mich.: Baker Book House, 1976.

Steere, Douglas. *Prayer and Worship*. New York: Association Press, 1938.

Teresa of Avila. *Living Water: Daily Reading with St. Teresa of Avila*. Edited by Sister Mary. London: Darton, Longman, and Todd Ltd., 1985.

Teresa of Avila. *The Soul's Passion for God: Selected Writings of Teresa of Avila*. Selected, edited, and introduced by Keith Beasley-Topliffe. Nashville, Tenn.: Upper Room Books, 1997.

Teresa of Jesus. *The Complete Works of Saint Teresa of Jesus*. Translated and edited by E. Allison Peers. London: Sheed & Ward, 1946.

Wicks, Robert J. *Seeds of Sensitivity: Deepening Your Spiritual Life*. Notre Dame, Ind.: Ave Maria Press, 1995

Willard, Dallas. *The Spirit of the Disciplines*. San Francisco: Harper and Row, Publishers, 1988.

A Year with the Saints. Translated by a Member of the Order of Mercy (Mt. St. Joseph's Seminary, Hartford, Conn.). Rockford, Ill.: Tan Books and Publishers, 1988.

God is "the boundless Abyss of all that is good, and sweet, and amiable." (William Law)

"God alone is that spring of love whose supply never fails." (Isaac of Syria)

(Week One)

From thee that I no more may stray,
No more thy goodness grieve,
Grant me the filial awe, I pray,
The tender conscience give.
Quick as the apple of an eye,
Oh God, my conscience make;
Awake my soul when sin is nigh,
And keep it still awake.
(Charles Wesley)

(Week Two)

"Attend to me. I am enough for you, and rejoice in your saviour and in your salvation." (Julian of Norwich)

(Week Three)

Our Father, who art in heaven,
hallowed be your name,
Your kingdom come,
Your will be done
on earth as it is in heaven.
Give us today our daily bread.
And forgive us our sins,
As we forgive those who sin against us.
Save us from the time of trial
and deliver us from evil.
For the Kingdom, the power, and the
    glory are yours
now and forever. Amen.
(International Consultation on English
    Texts)
(Week Four)

"Love has no more of pride than light has of darkness; it stands and bears all its fruits from a depth, and root of humility." (William Law)

(Week Five)

"Never fear that the Lord Who invites us to drink of the fountain will allow us to die of thirst." (Teresa of Avila)

(Week Seven)

Come, Saviour, come and make me
    whole,
Entirely all my sins remove;
To perfect health restore my soul,
To perfect holiness and love.
(Charles Wesley)

(Week Six)

Acknowledgments

This page constitutes a continuation of the copyright page. The publisher gratefully acknowledges the following copyright holders for permission to use copyrighted material:

The Very Reverend Nathan D. Baxter, Dean of the Washington National Cathedral, for excerpt from his sermon "Diane's Story, Our Story," 16 April 1995.

Jeannine C. Brabon for excerpts from her letter.

Darton, Longman & Todd for excerpts from *Living Water: Daily Readings with St. Teresa of Avila*, ed. by Sister Mary. Copyright © 1985 Sister Mary Eland.

Pauline J. Hord for excerpts from her letter.

International Consultation on English Texts for "The Lord's Prayer."

Karla M. Kincannon for excerpts from her funeral tribute to her grandmother.

Carol Kortsch for excerpts from her letter.

Mat, Cindy, and Jesse Anne Lipscomb for their story.

Paulist Press for excerpts from *Julian of Norwich: Showings*, trans. by Edmund Colledge and James Walsh. Copyright © 1978 by The Missionary Society of St. Paul the Apostle in the State of New York.

William A. Ritter for excerpts from his sermons: "Demons Out, Demons In," 21 February 1999, and "Table Manners," 17 February 1999.

James Rutenbeck for excerpts from his letter.

Sheed & Ward for excerpts from *The Complete Works of St. Teresa of Jesus*, trans. by E. Allison Peers. Copyright © 1946. Reprinted by permission of Sheed & Ward, an Apostolate of the Priests of the Sacred Heart. 7373 South Lover's Lane Road, Franklin, Wisconsin 53132 (414-529-6400) and Sheed & Ward (London).

Tan Books and Publishers for excerpts from *A Year with the Saints*. Rockford, Ill.: Tan Books and Publishers, 1988.

Templegate Publishers for excerpts from *The Joy of the Saints*, arr. by Robert Llewelyn. Springfield, Ill.: Templegate Publishers, 1989, and excerpts from *Daily Readings with Julian of Norwich*, vol. 1, trans. copyright © 1980 by The Julian Shrine. Springfield, Ill.: Templegate Publishers, 1989, and excerpts from *Living Water: Daily Readings with St. Teresa of Avila*, ed. by Sister Mary. Copyright © 1985 Sister Mary Eland.

Mark Trotter for excerpts from his sermon "What Is the Use?" 11 April 1999.

Austin Veleff for excerpts from his letter.

Tanya Denise Woodham for excerpts from her testimony.

Upper Room Spiritual Classics, Series 2

With this second set of devotional classics, Upper Room Books® offers selections from more great Christian writers — Francis and Clare, Julian of Norwich, Evelyn Underhill, Toyohiko Kagawa, and Thomas à Kempis.   ISBN# 0-8358-0853-X $24.00 (5 TITLES IN SLIPCASE)

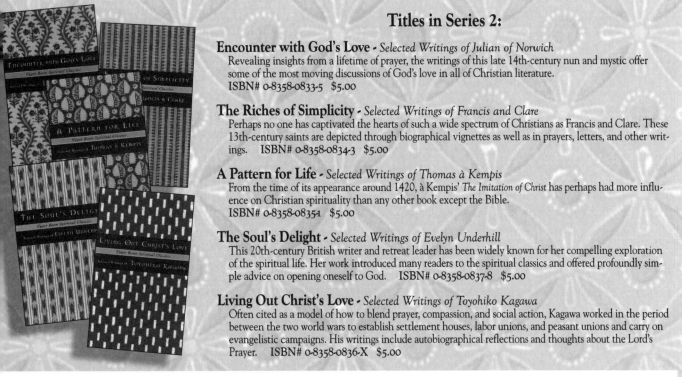

Titles in Series 2:

Encounter with God's Love - *Selected Writings of Julian of Norwich*
Revealing insights from a lifetime of prayer, the writings of this late 14th-century nun and mystic offer some of the most moving discussions of God's love in all of Christian literature. ISBN# 0-8358-0833-5 $5.00

The Riches of Simplicity - *Selected Writings of Francis and Clare*
Perhaps no one has captivated the hearts of such a wide spectrum of Christians as Francis and Clare. These 13th-century saints are depicted through biographical vignettes as well as in prayers, letters, and other writings.   ISBN# 0-8358-0834-3 $5.00

A Pattern for Life - *Selected Writings of Thomas à Kempis*
From the time of its appearance around 1420, à Kempis' *The Imitation of Christ* has perhaps had more influence on Christian spirituality than any other book except the Bible. ISBN# 0-8358-08351 $5.00

The Soul's Delight - *Selected Writings of Evelyn Underhill*
This 20th-century British writer and retreat leader has been widely known for her compelling exploration of the spiritual life. Her work introduced many readers to the spiritual classics and offered profoundly simple advice on opening oneself to God.   ISBN# 0-8358-0837-8 $5.00

Living Out Christ's Love - *Selected Writings of Toyohiko Kagawa*
Often cited as a model of how to blend prayer, compassion, and social action, Kagawa worked in the period between the two world wars to establish settlement houses, labor unions, and peasant unions and carry on evangelistic campaigns. His writings include autobiographical reflections and thoughts about the Lord's Prayer.   ISBN# 0-8358-0836-X $5.00

Upper Room Spiritual Classics, Series 3

This third set of devotional classics includes wisdom from spiritual leaders who strove to devote their lives totally to the will of God: John of the Cross, the Desert Mothers and Fathers, John Law, John Woolman, and Catherine of Siena.   ISBN# 0-8358-0905-6 $24.00 (5 TITLES IN SLIPCASE)

Titles in Series 3:

Loving God Through the Darkness - *Selected Writings of John of the Cross*
Loving God alone requires detachment from other things, a process of moving through the "dark night of the soul." John of the Cross elegantly expresses this process of seeking divine union in his poems and books on the spiritual life. A Carmelite monk and a close associate of Teresa of Avila, John lived during the religious turmoil of 16th-century Spain.   ISBN# 0-8358-0904-8 $5.00

Seeking a Purer Christian Life - *The Desert Mothers and Fathers*
In the third, fourth, and fifth centuries, thousands of men and women moved into the deserts of Egypt and Syria to seek a simple way of living. Their sayings about prayer, spiritual disciplines, and living in community spread throughout the Christian world and became the foundation of monasticism. ISBN# 0-8358-09021 $5.00

Total Devotion to God - *Selected Writings of William Law*
In these selections from his book *A Serious Call to a Devout and Holy Life*, Law calls for a total devotion to God. Responding to the religious moderation of 18th-century England, Law writes that the truly devout must live their lives in utter accordance with the will of God.   ISBN# 0-8358-0901-3 $5.00

Walking Humbly with God - *Selected Writings of John Woolman*
Woolman's *Journal* reveals the development of a Christian soul seeking to know and do God's will in all things. A devout Quaker, Woolman lived simply, in solidarity with the poor and oppressed. He traveled throughout the American colonies in the mid-1700s, urging other Quakers to free their slaves and to stand with him against slavery.   ISBN# 0-8358-0900-5 $5.00

A Life of Total Prayer - *Selected Writings of Catherine of Siena*
In seeking to submit her will completely to God, Catherine of Siena practiced extreme self-sacrifice fueled by prayer so intense that she often lost awareness of the world around her. She expressed these experiences in letters and writings that address the turbulent times of 14th-century Italy in which she lived. ISBN# 0-8358-0903-X $5.00